CATHOLIC GIRL
in the '50s

CATHOLIC GIRL
in the '50s

Mary Ellen Kauth Olsson

XULON PRESS

Xulon Press
2301 Lucien Way #415
Maitland, FL 32751
407.339.4217
www.xulonpress.com

Paperback ISBN-13: 978-1-66280-842-5

Ebook ISBN-13: 978-1-6628-0843-2

Table of Contents

Earliest Memories. 1

Meeting the Cathedral 6

The Dominican Regime 11

The Bishop's Church 39

Widening Our View 77

Friends Forever? 94

Somethings Old, Somethings New 97

Be Bop A Loo La 105

Sports, Speech, and Drama 124

He Ain't Heavy, Father, He's My Brother. . . . 130

Misbehaving in the 1950s and the Police 140

Ready or Not. 158

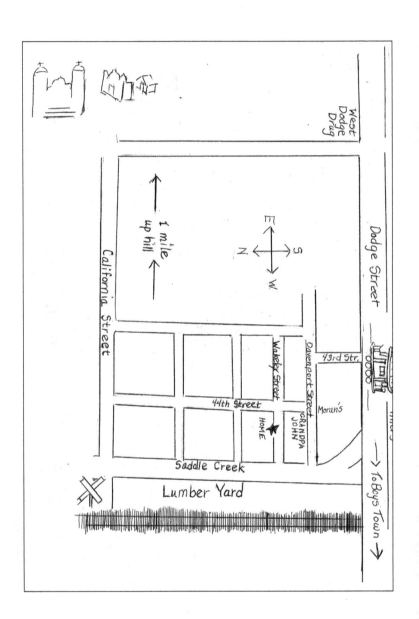

ACKNOWLEDGMENTS

A s I mentally walked down the streets of my childhood, the halls of my grade and high schools, and the aisle of my church, stories erupted that were long lost from my conscious mind. I wrote them down quickly, knowing facts were missing, names may be wrong, or the time frame may not fit. To help me with these oversights, I followed the direction of a nineteenth-century Teton chief who told his people, "I have seen in any great undertaking, it is not enough for a man to depend simply upon himself," and my family stepped up to help me develop a correct version of my tales.

I am so grateful for the help everyone gave to make our tales even more accurate and interesting. My children Robi, Matt, Nisi and Jere, maintained a mantra of support throughout my project. Michelle Synowicki and Mark Pleiss, thank you for reviewing my drafts and giving me your worthwhile comments and changes. Mark, a newly published author himself, helped me become aware of audience and publishing needs. Bert Pleiss, my wonderful sis, walked with me slowly through every story in this book, correcting wrong places, incorrect times, and catching every dangling participle. My special thanks also goes to my generous and talented husband who gave his time to proofread, provide technical assistance and refurbish 60 year old photographs with his Photoshop knowledge. And I cannot overlook Linda, Mary Ann, and Kay who listened with kind-

ness to my stories over and over again. I thank each and every one of you for sharing your genius with me on this project. You made the end product so much better. Oh, and I almost forgot to thank my co-writer, Polly. Your help was never fully appreciated, but thanks for the breaks.

PREFACE

As a former speech and drama coach, I recognize the importance of a setting as a backdrop to help the audience more easily recall the stories of that period. Therefore, my preface is designed to help the reader better understand life in the 1950s. In this decade, people were still in shock from the horrors of the 1940s: the cruelty of prison camps and needless Jewish deaths, the numbers of American family members killed on foreign soil, the dropping of the A bombs on Japan, and more dying in the Korean War. People were tired of war and hungry for peace. The backdrop for my "Catholic Girl" stories was one of change.

World War II had robbed most American towns of normal growth and development because of the allocation of funds and rationing of supplies during those years. Omaha suffered as well, so when the soldiers returned to their hometown from battle-fields around the world, they stepped back into a familiar scene, but cities filled with joy.

Uncle Jack (my mom's brother and an honored parachute soldier) and great-grandpa Bob (my dad) returned to the celebratory parades of the city and the rejoicing of their families. My father's dad (great-great-grandpa Fred) worked in the city hall building, and his office window balcony served as a perfect seat to watch the countless parades. We watched Uncle Jack, the post-war commander of the American Legion, carrying the flag at the beginning of each parade, honoring all returning soldiers of Omaha. This city couldn't have been more proud. Little did we know the changes that came home with these returning victors.

During the war, gas was being rationed, and few people could buy a car, so the city transportation system was very popular in the 1940s and '50s. It consisted of an electrical streetcar system connecting the Omaha suburbs of Benson, Dundee, and Florence to downtown Omaha. My mother's father (Great-Great-Grandpa John) was a streetcar engineer when the cars were pulled by horses, but in 1950s, the electric car carried commuters from all over town to their destinations.

I have fond memories the insistent tink-a-link bell screaming, and the streetcar clacking as it moved from stop to stop in the middle of the busiest streets. Although the woven straw seats pinched my legs as I sat in my dress, the ride was always special, and I was saddened to see the streetcar era end. In 1955, car #1011 rolled to its final stop. Brick streets were replaced and tracks removed throughout the city as the bus became the favorite mode of city transportation.

Other changes came to Omaha when the G.I. Bill became available for the returning soldiers, and it brought money into the community. New tracks of look-alike housing mushroomed up around the city, and the returning soldiers were given low-interest mortgages. New businesses opened and serviced Omaha, and tech schools and universities were enlarged to accommodate those soldiers using the G.I. Bill stipends for education. Women, who had left the home to support the war effort and work in places like the Bomber Plant south of Omaha, returned to their families, and the returning soldiers took their places. Roller skating, big bands, ballroom dancing, eating out, and movies became entertainment again. Fun had returned to the streets of Omaha.

City politics remained similar to the way they were prewar, as the city bosses continued to tear down historic buildings, such as the classic post office and city hall. My young heart bled when I saw the *Omaha World Herald*'s pictures of the stone statues, decorative relief, and classic beauty of those beautiful buildings on the ground. It seemed these city fathers wanted nothing to do with the past and tried to remove it with the wrecking ball. Nationally, the politics appeared to be the same conservative approach with the election of a Republican war hero, General Dwight D. Eisenhower, but this new president's military thinking brought new design to our country.

During his eight years, the US experienced many changes and beginnings:

- Hawaii and Alaska were now considered strategic to US safety and were brought into full statehood;
- The Interstate Highway System was initiated, allowing quick movement of military machines if needed;
- 1957 Civil Rights Acts were passed which led to the Civil Rights Commission;
- NASA was created as another form of US security and the space administration team was established;
- "Atoms for Peace" was presented at the UN General Assembly as a design for the future;
- Warning of the "Cold War, Military-Industrial Complex" was a constant mantra in military planning; and
- All school children practiced head-hiding positions under their desks or in windowless

rooms, rehearsing for the possible bombing of our cities.

As a child, I did not fully realize the newness that Ike caused in our lives; I just remember hearing "I Like Ike" around our Democratic home.

Families were able to attend church together again, and church building and attendance increased. Omaha had evolved from a naughty little river town to a metropolis, and in the post war, it trumpeted a variety of religious beliefs, churches, and synagogues. The little ethnic communities of Omaha had already become a cultural world of their own, centering around their churches, and many of these communities were of a Catholic denomination, so the numbers of Omaha Catholics grew.

In the nineteenth century, a need and desire for an archdiocesan cathedral evolved, and plans began to develop. Ground became available near 40th and Cummings Street (40th and Dewey). Although many Catholics thought the land was too far west, being forty blocks west of the Missouri

River, construction began in 1907, and it was completed in 1959 with towers crowned, new statues in place, and the last brick laid. All of Omaha celebrated its completion, and St. Cecilia students were a part of every celebratory event.

This beautiful Spanish Renaissance structure with imported art, parquet marble flooring, renowned colored-glass windows, and resounding organ housed the 1960 class's every celebration and sacrament and was almost considered commonplace for the students who had it in their life daily. Our youthful attention seldom recognized the beauty and spiritual guidance built into the structure we saw every day.

When writing my memories in the "Chimes," the Omaha Cathedral newsletter, I called the column, "Herkie Remembers ..." and I am often asked why that name and where I got it. My usual answer was that my mom called me "Herkie" when she carried me, not knowing my sex before I was born. (She painted Herkie's bed, or bought cloth diapers for Herkie). Friends that I have grown up with or played with call me, "Herkie," and later friends shortened it to "Herk," but the stories that follow are "Herkie" stories.

EARLIEST MEMORIES

S ome days when I walk into a different room, I forget what I came for, but ironically I have a surprisingly clear memory of the past. Our only grandchild, Iliya-Kenny, is being raised in Bulgaria and will not know our family stories without my transcript. I have begun writing our stories for him and calling upon my gift of memory to develop this book.

My earliest memories are of my mom, dad, and me living with Grandpa John on the corner of 44th and Davenport Streets of Omaha, Nebraska, in the mid-1940s. My playground was my Grandpa John's large backyard with a swing set for my play, and bird feeders to watch. All birds were welcome except "spatsies" (or sparrows, Grandpa John's most-hated bird). When I tired of playing in the backyard, I could bury myself in the plants of Grandpa's garden and eat fresh peas, or I could climb in the fruit trees on the south side of the house and entertain a too-much-fruit stomach ache.

When I was feeling brave, I would slowly, slowly step down the steep stairs to the dug-out basement under the house. The dark, damp air always made bumps on my arms, and big, black water bugs would scurry to safety on the dirt floor. They crunched when you stepped on them, so I always wore shoes when my mother sent me down to fetch her canned fruit or vegetables that stood waiting on the shelves.

During the summer and fall seasons, all activity centered around Grandpa's garden goods and fruit produce for our table. From June to October, my mom's kitchen was a bubbling, steaming, hot pot with thick, inviting smells. Her apron would clean counters, wipe off fruit, and mop her forehead. Seldom a day went by that there wasn't a line of clean clothes flapping in the wind and whitening in the sun. The next morning, a clean apron would protect her cotton dress as yesterday's apron flapped happily on the clothesline.

My dad's arrival home from Europe and World War II, my sister's birth, and my own growth made it apparent that Grandpa's two-bedroom house was getting too small for us all. My mom wanted to stay close to her dad so she could continue to help Grandpa John, so the search for our new home was limited to Cathedral Parish neighborhoods. The Arnold's house went up for sale a half a block away from Grandpa's, and my parents were soon moving boxes and unused furniture to 4404 Wakeley Street.

This new address turned a new page of life for me in many ways: a brand-new, exciting world with a new home, new kids to play with—and I started school!

MEETING THE CATHEDRAL

Our destination every Sunday morning was St. Cecilia's Cathedral on 40th and Webster Streets. The church was named after Saint Cecilia, the patron of music, and was built in the Spanish Medieval tradition on the highest hill on the outskirts of this pioneer town. When construction was started on the huge church in 1905, Omahans shook their heads at the decision to build one of the largest cathedrals on that spot, fearing it was too far west for the city. In the 1930s, a lack of funds temporarily halted progress, but a door-to-door canvas brought money into the coffers once more, and in the 1950s, the twin spires stretched unfinished high into the sky, visible to all within the city limits. The towers were finally completed in 1959.

Most families from Wakeley Street were involved in this weekly pilgrimage each Sunday, usually for the

11:15 Mass. Although the neighbors had shouted, "Good morning" just fifteen minutes before from their driveways, they nodded, waved, or whispered, "Hello" again as they were getting into the pews of the huge church.

As a little person coming to church with my parents, the unforgiving marble steps were difficult for short little legs. The bronze handrails meant to assist were at first out of reach, but eventually became more and more helpful. Then we faced the challenge of the heavy metal doors. Even for my dad or any adult, the huge, beautiful bronze doors opened slowly, but it was well worth the struggle when you saw the view behind them. The bright lights glared down on marble parquet flooring between the shiny oak pews.

Once behind the heavy doors, you would hear the organ calling us to join our community. The 1950s was before the ecumenical crowd participation, so we were primarily an audience. If we were lucky, the choir that was housed with the organ in the majestic Romanesque edifice in the elevated rear of the church would also sing.

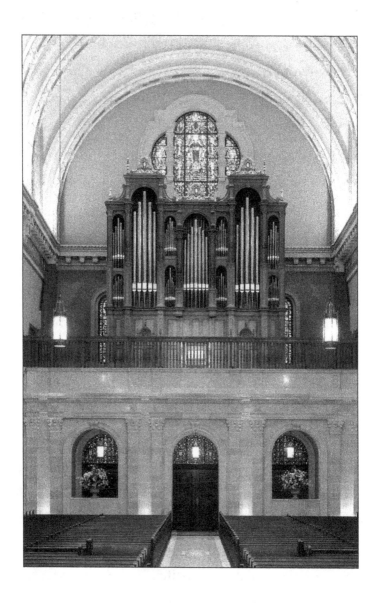

If you have web access, you can hear the cathedral organ being played by today's director, Dr. Marie Bauer. Enter the following address: https//vimeo.com 468837634 Once in the vimeo website and looking at the trees, click on the center of the picture.

In the '50s, few organists took the reins of the organ in the cathedral. Even as a young student, I recognized Mrs. F's guidance. Her regime was rigorous and controlled as she executed the sacred treasury of music for each archdiocesan celebration. At each celebration, we enjoyed that magnificent organ and its master, filling that huge church with prayerful music.

My parents always sat toward the back of the church, with me sitting next to the aisle. My eyes would follow the very long path between the pews to the white marble altar reaching up the East wall. And there it was, the bigger-than-life cross with a bigger-than-life golden body of Christ looking up to His Father.

Little did I know how many times I would walk down that aisle in my lifetime. My parents, Bob and Lill, were married in the cathedral in 1940, and they brought their firstborn (me) for baptism in 1942. But throughout my life, I walked down that very aisle for each successive sacrament or event: First Communion, Confession, Confirmation, Safety and Fire Patrol Acknowledgment, Honor Society, eighth-grade graduation, high school graduation, teacher acknowledgment, my marriage, baptism of my children, as well as the hundreds of times throughout the years that as students, we welcomed the bishop in procession.

THE DOMINICAN REGIME

C atholic education at this time did not include the financial investment as is required today. My sister's and my education had no formal tuition, but it was not free; it was actually dependent upon Sunday and special collections from parents and parish members to maintain the buildings and procure books. The moans and complaints would belch up from our dad at special collection times and permeate our house for about a week around the volunteer's visit, but he would always dig deep into his pockets because he knew the quality education his girls were getting from the Dominican sisters. He even became a volunteer for several years, which had him visiting homes for a month, a long commitment for our father.

Besides parish donations, our private education was possible at this price because of the sisters. The commitment from the Dominican sisters from the Mound in Southeast Wisconsin promised a certain number of teaching nuns for a meager stipend and housing for the sisters. Although their convent on the outside did not reflect the vow of poverty they took at their profession, their monthly income did. These professional, well-educated women worked for very little money in their promise to lead their students to God and a purposeful life.

I remember seeing my first Dominican sister in the traditional habit, rather frightening for a first grader. I watched carefully as this strangely dressed person welcomed my mom and me into my new school room. I watched every move of this creature, trying to determine whether it was a "he" or a "she." No hair apparent to give a clue; it was under a white cap covering the head and neck. No breast bulges were apparent; no make-up, just shiny skin, bushy eye brows, and white teeth showed, and they were gender neutral. The only clue I had was that my mother called her "Sister" and my sister was a girl, so Sister was a she.

The head piece, the veil, floor-length dress, and scapular covered all body parts except face and hands, and we were always trying to see something that showed their womanhood. It was always fun to see Sister hike her skirts to run to first base in our baseball game and show her legs clothed with black silk stockings and old-lady shoes.

There was another time, a rather awkward time, when I was seated toward the front of the class with my head down while Sister was reading a story. I remember that she paused between sentences, catching my attention, and then she emphatically turned up her volume with her next word and gesture. When I raised my eyes, I was looking up the sleeve of her outstretched arm. I could not stop looking. What I saw confirmed our suspicions; Sister wore Fruit of the Loom t-shirts for underwear—and Sister did not shave under her arms! I shut my eyes; I knew my glimpse was forbidden. Sister and I had shared something very personal, and she did not even know.

The Dominican regime was rigorous, and all the sisters were strict, striking the fear of God in us for this or for that, but there were also many teachers in my time at Cathedral, who melted my heart and stimulated my learning. My first-grade teacher was one of them. Loving stories about this little nun preceded our experience, and all of us were excited. We had heard from our neighbors and older siblings that she was nice and loved small people. She was also known to have magical powers in her hugs, healing all hurts and boo-boos just by enclosing you in her embrace. Her arms would surround you, she would pull you into all that white cloth, and whatever was hurting would dissolve away as you became a part of her fabric.

That summer before school started seemed to crawl more slowly than it ever had, but finally the day arrived. We all stood in our first line outside the small portable building behind the tall elementary building. At last the door opened, and twenty-three five-year-olds turned to welcome this special, round little lady in traditional Dominican garb. She seemed only a little taller than us, and her smile and kind words welcomed us and almost dissolved our fears of leaving our moms, as she led us through the large wooden doors to whatever lay behind.

This new little class filled our clean-smelling classroom, and we were assigned seats in the rows of newly polished oak desks whose folding seats stood at attention until we sat in them. Little did we know, the majority of this busy little group would become friends, complete cathedral's elementary and secondary regime and graduate together twelve years later. The life time of friendship was not envisioned by this wiggly, giggly, non-stop talking bunch, but Sister M. saw the bigger picture and accepted the responsibility in our journey and began nurturing our path.

That first day I learned so many things. We learned the bathroom was a "lavatory," and we could go to the lavatory at 10:00, after lunch, and at 2:00. We learned we would hang our coats and store our lunches in something called a "cloak closet" where everyone had their own hook. I saw big, colorful pictures that rolled up and down above the chalk-board. I learned that we would keep our Big Tablets, new pencils, and erasers that we brought from home in a clever shelf under our desktops.

I learned that the ink hole in my desktop could hurt my hand if I put it in it, but it fit my hand just per-fectly. I learned that the big stick next to Sister's desk, bigger than Sister, was used to open windows from the top for more air. It was a lot to remember.

On the second day, however, an insect changed my image of first grade, and my real learning began. It was a very hot day in August in 1948, and Sister M. was doing everything to keep our non-air-conditioned classroom cool. Her adoring class watched the little nun as she made the gadget on the end of the long stick pull down the top section of the windows for better air circulation. It was on the last window pull that we saw "*it*" fly through the new opening. No matter what Sister did to regain our attention, the entire class could not take their eyes off the giant bumble bee as it slowly circled high above us.

As its circle of flight became wider and wider, the chatter among us louder and more interesting, until even the most attentive of us lost interest in the bee.

Realizing our focus had left the bee, Sister instructed us to sit down and get back to work. We all dutifully followed her instructions, and we slid our way back into our newly varnished seats. My scream cut through the room noise as I popped out of my desk shocking all. My cries got louder, and my antics continued. Oh, my bottom burned, and my screams continued as I grabbed my behind, dancing to my own music.

Instead of the warm empathy I expected from Sister, I received a strong reprimand for my noise and was told to sit down and quit acting like a baby. I pushed aside the body of the bumble bee (they die if you sit on them), and obediently lowered myself onto my throbbing butt cheek, gulping air in an attempt to breathe. Concentration on my work was more than I could give. My head lowered onto my desk, and eventually my uneven gasps for air began to lessen. First grade, long sticks with hooks, Sister M., and bumblebees were never the same.

Sister didn't mean to give me this vivid memory so many years later. Becoming strict in a momentary crisis was her only strategy to regain crowd control and silence her young students, necessary in her mind for learning.

Most of the teachers in the 1950s were sisters, but when the mother house could not allocate the number of sisters needed for all classes, an advertisement went out for what they called "lay teachers." These teachers were to be certified, working on certification or their degree, or have an emergency certificate. The sisters were given a small stipend for their work, and the lay teacher was given half of what their public school peer was making, and they received no retirement or health care benefits.

As a lay teacher at Cathedral for a number of years, I chose these payment oversights in trade for the wonderful people with whom I taught, the terrific students, the autonomy and respect I was given, and the true purpose and direction both teachers and students claimed. Though you never felt quite on the level of the sisters, your work was appreciated and supported by parish and parents alike.

One of these lay teachers taught our class in the upstairs of the old Barmettler home on the north end of the football practice field. They nailed some old ink well desks to the second floor of this house, and Mrs. "S's" desk was at the front of the room. She was a soft-spoken, gentle lady who obviously enjoyed us and her profession, and her handling of misbehavior was in keeping with her nature.

Her strategy for student misbehavior involved a new pencil with an eraser and a permanent ink pad. When a student broke any classroom rule, (talking out of turn, leaving your seat without permission, passing notes—my usual sins), she would not yell, nor hit our hands with a ruler or even call home. She would quietly call you forward to her desk, slowly open the drawer by her tummy and remove the new pencil and ink pad. She would then rub the end of the eraser in the fresh ink and put a (almost) permanent circle on your nose. If your nose was already housing a black spot (which so many times mine was), she would move to the next available spot on your face. Some of us would go home sporting many of these "black freckles," and the permanent nature of the ink announced to your parents the level of cooperation you had given that day. Neither human spit nor washroom soap would relieve us of our apparent guilt, and this was the day and age that parents supported the teacher and administration without question. The wrath that those little spots brought into our second grade lives was significant and behavior-changing for most of us.

A fun note to this story involves Mrs. S's retirement after forty-two years of service. This author was teaching at St. Cecilia's when the retirement party was announced, and I was asked to speak since I was a peer who once had been her student. Writing this speech was not difficult, and enumerating the special nature of this lady who had given so much for so many years was an easy task. The irony of my talk was at the end of my speech when from beneath the podium, I withdrew a new pencil and an ink pad—and well, you know the rest. Mrs. S. got her first black mark. Gosh, that felt good.

At our reunions, sometimes our memories churn up stories of unhappy school experiences, and today we laugh and rejoice in our survival. Not many, but some sisters did not enjoy children. Although these teachers had the conscious intention of making their students godly, sometimes they were unable to deal with the stresses of the classroom. These teachers may have been overzealous disciplinarians, disregarding special needs, grading without concern, or even utilizing corporal punishment for misbehavior. These were certainly not the norms at St. Cecilia's, but occasionally a teacher struggling to control her class unfairly appeared.

I always prided myself in recognizing this type of teacher. The configuration of the veil proved to be quite an accurate analysis of each sister's nature. The veil of the traditional Dominican habit had a rounded, barrel form from a pin at the top of the head to her shoulders. The Sister whose veil was open and hanging as designed was usually kind and patient. When the veil's sides were damaged, it was usually indicative of a trigger temper whose wrath usually fell on her students. In her frustration with our behavior or lack of scholastic success, she would push her veil back like a ponytail, damaging its designed structure. After the first school quarter of treating the veil this way, the stiffening was damaged, and the veil would hang lifeless behind her shoulders. If in the hall, I saw a limp, misshaped veil, I would duck into the nearest classroom or cloakroom for fear of the temperament of the lady wearing it.

My third-grade experience involved a very strict sister who never smiled and who wore a veil that fell to her shoulders, limp and broken. I knew, when I saw her veil, it was not going to be a fun year, and as the year passed, my misery grew. One morning, my mother received a call from the secretary at school. She reported that I had not arrived and wondered if I was ill (few schools do that anymore). My mother told them that she had sent me off at the routine time and that I should be there by now. Mom retraced my usual path and found me sitting on a corner curb crying. Feeling my mother's warmth and concern as we sat on that curb together allowed my fear of this teacher and class-room happenings to belch out of me between sobs.

I told Mom that I didn't want to go back there; I told her that Sister was mean. My bot-tled-up fears broke loose, and out they came. I boldly went on slightly fearful because our parents, like so many parents of that time, never took our side when we brought complaints home, and there I was telling on a sister. Surprisingly, Mom walked me hand-in-hand to school and to the principal's office, reassuring me all the way that all would be well.

Fear rushed in again as I sat outside the principal's office while my mother visited with the her behind the closed door. The hands of the large clock took my attention and I watched them slowly move—click, click. After what seemed forever, they were still talking as they left the office. I was ignored by both adults when they finally joined me, but my hand was taken again, and the three of us walked up the stairs together.

Each step pumped my anxiety higher. I expected my mother to disappear at any time, feeling satisfied that she had done her motherly job, but she stayed. Her presence helped my fear that I was about to be thrown into the clutches of the beast that knew she had been betrayed.

Everyone knew that I had ratted, and now they knew I was a baby that needed her mommy too.

Although I could hardly move, I kept my crying inside me. I didn't cling to my mother's skirts, and bravely walked into the classroom, took my seat, and prayed while my mother and Sister Principal talked to the Beast in the hall. None of my fears of death or torture materialized, of course, and my mother winked goodbye once she knew that I was safe. I continued my day's work.

What really happened after the incident was not anywhere as dramatic as my imagination had taken me. Sister L's tenor toward me was more of ignoring me than great modifications in the way she treated me. She still would not accept an answer as correct if I had not placed a period at the end of the sentence; dress codes were still law; silence was the only environment in her classroom; and she still expected her long assignments to be perfect (no recess until the grade was 100 percent using flawless Palmer method of writing). Her severe, restrictive list still haunted our learning atmosphere, but I seemed now to be out of the cross hairs for her snap judgment and cruel comments.

She was my third grade teacher, and I don't have to tell you the joy I felt on the last day of that school year. And you can probably also imagine my hopelessness when in July they notified my family that I had been assigned to a split room of third and fourth with the *same* teacher!

My familiar stomach ache returned with the thought of another year like the last. But with a little more maturity on my part, and Sister's understanding of my sensitivities, we both made it through my fourth-grade year without incident—at least nothing so intense as to make it into these notes, or maybe it was just a blur.

Fifth grade put our class on the second floor of the big, brick building. It was built in a time when oak was the finest building material for walls, floors, doors, and furniture. Our desks and Sister's desk matched the wooden, wide-planked floor of our room and the steps and banisters that led to it. Florescent lights and big windows brightened this fifth-grade classroom. One day, while we were working quietly, a loud "crack" called us out of our concentration. Our eyes quickly wandered to the ceiling, looking for the cause when another loud crack showed us the direction. A stream of hot, green liquid fell from the light by the cloak room upon an unaware student. Sister rushed her out of the room and returned without her, and I don't remember the student ever returning to class. Sister never did tell us what had happened (she probably wasn't sure either). We knew to pray for her.

When you were in fifth or sixth grade, the sisters started giving us more responsibility. We were taught, now that we were growing up, it was our job to make a positive difference wherever we were. We became crossing guards, hall monitors, and Fire Patrol members. We also shared what we were studying in science and math with younger classes, and any projects we were doing were put in the hall for other classes to see. We also went to the primary rooms and read with the younger students in their textbooks and story books.

Sister would enter us in contests outside the classroom as well. We would write an essay or poem, or draw a picture, and Sister would send them to a magazine, post it on the bulletin boards or enter it in the appropriate contest. One October weekend in 1953, the Fire Patrol members were invited to attend a free movie and treats at the Orpheum Theater in downtown Omaha, and the Fire Prevention poster contest winners were to be announced. It had been some time since the Fire Patrol volunteers had finished the posters we entered, so I initially did not respond when my name was called. I had won first place in the city-wide contest! (My poster read, "Most Fires Start from Scratch; Use Care," and it had a very big match stick starting to ignite.) My $25.00 prize money was spent quickly, and my radio alarm clock sits in storage somewhere, but the self-esteem perk I got from sharing my work and the response it received is still alive and well in my life.

My sixth-grade class was on the third floor, and this classroom had wonderful magic. It was filled with an abundance of Sister's caring, love, and of course instruction. We knew she liked us and liked teaching us. She would crouch down next to our desk if we needed help, and when something tickled her, her laughter would mushroom up and fill the room. Many times we would join the fun, not knowing why we were laughing.

We always celebrated when we completed the units on which we were working, and Sister and our cupcake-making moms made it a party. Sister loved having fun, and wanted us to have fun in our work, so she implemented activities that stimulated thought and lots of work.

One example was when we finished our units, we were given a period at the end of the next Friday's schedule. It wasn't free time; however, we were allowed to take a thirty-minute break at the end of the week and entertain each other with a prepared song, dance, mime, or presentation. We chose our partner or group; selected our material; planned the choreography, costumes, and props; and then we would rehearse, rehearse, rehearse.

Finally, we would tell Sister we were ready for our theatrical debut.

It was our turn to perform, and the date was set. After weeks of preparation, sleepless nights of anxiety, and arguments within our group, we would sit and wait for those Friday hours to tick away (If no one had prepared something that week, or if we had not completed our units, we would just continue our work, so everyone worked hard and gladly took their turn and recruited any willing soul to help.)

Treats were allowed during this half hour (another motivator) which turned our thirty-minute break into a party. Some of the frothiest homemade cupcakes or boxes of chocolate chip or oatmeal raisin cookies baked by our stay-at-home moms walked in with us on those Fridays. "The treats will wait in the cloakroom until time," Sister would say.

When work was checked, and it was our time to entertain, we assumed our places, and a secret sign alerted our musical assistant to ready the large record player. The light blinked on the front of the player, and the machine screeched in readiness. The music began, and our fear melted away. After hours and hours of rehearsing our every turn and gesture and correctly mouthing the words emanating from the 78 rpm record. "I broke my bat on Johnny's head, someone snitched on me," we mouthed the words of the modern Christmas carol and twisted and turned with perfect timing. The five minutes of entertainment seemed like five seconds. Before we knew it, we were happily munching on our chocolate cupcakes with sprinkles. Our debut was a success, and Sister began looking for the next group. I don't know what our Iowa Basic Tests said about us that year, but I know we learned a lot.

Hormones kicked in in the seventh and eighth grades, and a new perspective entered our lives. Boys no longer gagged when asked to sit next to a girl or have her on his team; girls now welcomed the attention that used to irritate them. Some girls were plumping out in the chest, and it was clear we were growing out of the blue bib uniforms and getting ready for the green vests the girls wore in the high school across the street. Boys couldn't sing like they used to, and their faces were developing pink splotches and hair. The sisters had lost control of some of this new interaction between girl and boy students in their classes, and their attempt to regain it resembled someone herding cats.

Although seventh and eighth grades (junior high) was really no different than other school years at St. Cecilia's, the dynamics growing within the students made the difference. "Girlfriends and boyfriends" were becoming a common thing. The sisters dealt with this change with what they called "dances," which meant we could dance to music chosen by the sisters in the grade school cafeteria after school about once a month.

Certain musicians were considered sinful, I guess, because there was censure in the music selection. (I did not know much about Elvis until late high school when my public school friends had been screaming and dancing to his music for years.) Slow songs allowed the budding boyfriends and girlfriends to dance two feet apart to the selected music. Dancing as a couple in front of the rest of the class was exciting for the girl or boy and, of course, their friends. Giggles and blushing faces seemed to spread across the room in waves, as one brave soul after another walked across the divide to ask his choice to dance.

Walking home after the dance was almost as much fun. Our dances only lasted about an hour (one and a half hours if a parent made treats), so the giggling and laughter continued as we skipped, ran, and continued the fun down the hills to home. "He likes you," my friend would shout. "No, he doesn't" would be my response. "Herkie and Joey sitting in a tree," my friend would sing, " k-i-s-s-i-n-g—Ha Ha," and the giggling would continue.

A uniform change happened when the girls crossed the street to attend high school. At first, it was exciting. The blue bibbed, pleated-skirt model of the grade school uniform was replaced with the vested, green-skirted, two-piece version. As time passed, the girls hated both uniforms, and as hard as we tried to destroy them, they never went away. We actually thought their threads were made of steel, as the holes we poked would disappear, and we couldn't even frazzle the edges of the fabric. They seemed to survive any intentional mistreatment and instead became hand-me-downs to younger students.

After the call from Brandeis on 16th and Douglas Streets in downtown Omaha announcing the arrival of our uniform order, my mother, my sister, and I rode the bus or streetcar (like a lot of ladies at this time, my mother never drove) to pick up our uniforms and two or three blouses. Not only was this usually a one-time purchase of clothing for the year, but thanks to an ample hem, steel threads, and the creativity of those Catholic moms, growth spurts were successfully addressed for its first owner, and then passed on into its second and third life.

For moms who didn't sew, the end of each year resembled a food frenzy with fast and furious phone calls, seeking outgrown uniforms that looked like new. I have always believed that the uniforms we wore in the 1950s are probably laying in wait in some landfill, ready to wear today.

The uniformity required for the girls' attire was not demanded for the boys. For them, there were no defined uniforms, no orders from Brandeis, no fitting sessions and little hand-me-down action to little brothers. The handbook of the '50s gave boys their restrictions: no Levis (popular jeans thought to be wild), instead loose-fitting trousers were required (some said your shoes had to pass through the leg), and a dress shirt or a regulation sport shirt (button-down shirts were the norm).

Although the girls hated the monotony of the same dress each day— what we thought was unattractive—the uniform did have benefits we did not realize. Once we were parents buying school clothes, we realized the money our parents saved. Our uniforms cost around $28.00 and about $6.00 per blouse back then, a real bargain for a complete year. Today's research shows other benefits: behavior modification happens more easily when students are not competing in dress, all income levels are dressed the same, and scholastic focus seems to be easier.

THE BISHOP'S CHURCH

S t. Cecilia's is considered the bishop's church, and in the 1950s, almost any celebration with the bishop included a High Mass (very long), a body of parish priests and deacons from all over the city, and Cathedral students in procession. A rolling roar from the organ high in the loft announced the start, and we all stood up straight in readiness. An altar boy in a celebratory red-and-white cassock carried a gold cross as he led the procession to the altar. Other altar boys, also dressed in red cassocks, preceded the long line of girls with hands folded in their long white dresses. The flower girls, tossing their pedals to the ground, led the smelly incense bearer, visiting priests, deacons, and bishop who carried a big staff and wore a pointed hat.

Processions down that aisle were frequent enough that we would outgrow our white dress, and when hem-letting out did not suffice, another had to be made or purchased. The ten shortest girls in first grade and kindergarten were assigned the "flower girl" positions. Because of our height, my friend and I were flower girls, with all of those first grade students, right up into fifth grade, not much hem work had to be done on our dresses.

Each procession day was a wonderful time, but even for an adult, it was a terribly long, long commitment. Usually we met at 7:30 in the cafeteria for last-minute adjustments by the sisters who lined us up and marched us over to the back of the church.

The powerful organ announced our arrival. The processing in and out took time, and the bishop's mass challenged our sitting-still ability. When Mass was finally finished and we had escorted the pageant members out into the fresh air, the freedom was unbelievable. After three hours of sitting still, never slumping, trying to keep silent, and inhaling all that incense, my friend, "C.," and I would twist and twirl in our long, white dresses to music only she and I could hear as we danced back home.

A Child in the Big Church

But as grade school students in the 1950s, anytime we were in church, we found controlling our hands, feet, and mouth a difficult youthful endeavor. The sisters wanted us to attend daily Mass and made that invitation regularly. Sister, however, did not like little-people movements or secret-telling whispers, and the correction was made with a gun-sounding crack of a finger snap from the pew behind. If the behavior did not cease, a second finger snap would magically make the offender disappear from his/her place and reappear next to Sister where all freedom ceased.

Who could stop being us? I always thought Sister was asking the impossible of the young bodies in her care. Controlling ourselves, however, was only one of the problems we had as young Mass attendants in the '50s. There were other confusing elements when we went to daily church. For example, that tall, marble altar that stretched up also kept Father's back to us, and we couldn't see what he was doing. He was also speaking a language we did not know. Latin was the language of any Roman Catholic celebration, but none of us understood it, and we were expected to answer him in this language. The only other time we were able to vocalize in church was occasionally when the organ would rare up, pump to attention, and then soften, allowing our voices to join in prayerful song.

Self-control again became our master when the organ stopped, and we were left with our inner voices and visual wanderings. So my eyes would survey the marble altar with its large golden candelabras and candles that never seemed to burn down but flickered their light on the golden cross. Father occasionally turned around and spoke that language again, and thankfully, Sister had taught us how to say our response. My eyes would then wander to the wooden carved apostles that stood at attention around the pulpit, where Father talked to us about the gospel. My eyes would then follow the circular path to the large bishop's chair that never seemed to have an occupant except when I wore my white dress.

If our class was seated farther back in the church, the horizon was broader. My eyes would look up into the half-barrel ceiling with Jesus as King and angels appearing to live high in the sky. I wondered how in the world they got up there, or if they were paintings, who painted them and what kind of a ladder did they use? How did they know how big the hands should be, or how did they know what angels looked like? I never knew that Jesus was so big that He could hold our whole world in His one hand. How did they know that? All these questions floated around in my youthful head as I was trying to sit still. I would pray for a while, but then the questions would rush back. When I was tired of no answers, my eyes would move to the real dangers in church, those big hanging lights. I decided they looked too heavy to be dangling on those thin chains over our heads. I never sat under them unless there was no choice.

Pathways to Godliness

Sacraments, Plenary Indulgence, Spiritual Bouquets, Novenas, Litany of the Saints

The Dominican sisters in the 1950s and our families taught us the different paths to God in private prayer and public prayer. Our private prayer transpired between God and us individually, and activities of the church and school provided our outward prayer in Masses, sacraments, and procession. My grandmother would say the Memorial and Novena prayers as a morning ritual each day using her stack of holy cards about two inches tall. Our parents prayed the rosary privately, and each of us had a rosary. Any area of need told to our parents was welcomed and we all prayed for those privately. We saw our family members in their private prayer, and it became our practice as well.

In this form of prayer, I was usually asking for my grandpa's health or for some particular toy (but when prayer never brought me a new red bike, I realized God probably wasn't into granting gift wishes—but I tried). Rote prayers, blessed medals around your neck, prayer books, rosary beads, holy cards, statues in homes, church, and yards all stimulated our private prayer to our God or favorite saint.

I did not always understand the different ways to pray, but I would diligently say the Miraculous Heart of Mary prayer for those who had died, the Novena to St. Theresa for some intention that I thought no one would consider too menial, or prayers to St. Jude (the patron of impossible cases) for the most difficult intention. I was usually asking or begging for help to change what I considered the hard times in life.

On Mission Sunday, priests servicing and spreading the faith in Third World countries would visit our churches, and in their stumbling English would ask for our prayers and money after telling us stories of their very poor parishioners. Few people could resist reaching into their pockets for the last of their change. But alas, Mission prayer cards left in the pews told us the address of the Mother House for a further donations and prayers.

"Spiritual Bouquets" were another avenue to greater prayer in our lives, and were great gifts. Sister would help us decorate our home-made card displaying our collection of prayers, forming a bouquet for our mother or father. "This is the best gift you can give your mom," Sister would say. All I can say is that my mom displayed my handmade card like a piece of art and was always very happy with her bouquet.

When we were older in our understanding of God and the Church; venial and mortal sin; and heaven, hell, and purgatory; we moved into a different level of prayer. Novenas, always appreciated by my grandma, were now coming into my life. When an intention was deemed worthy of serious prayer, the prayer on the Novena card was read in a routine manner daily, followed by a certain number of certain prayers said at the same time of the day for nine days.

At church celebrations, a litany was a part of the ceremony called "Exposition of the Eucharist." This is when a large host of unleavened bread, believed to be the Body of Christ, is taken out of the tabernacle and put into a highly decorated monstrance that allows everyone to see it, revere it and pray for intentions. Usually the priests would sing or say a very long list of names of saints, followed by "Pray for Us" as a response from the congregation. It opened our awareness to the number of good people deemed "saints" and to whom we could pray in our Novenas and daily prayers. Most of the names we did not recognize, but we would repeat "Pray for us" again and again, hoping whoever it was would hear our prayer and help us.

Heaven and hell were a main concern of all our spiritual leaders, even in our elementary years. I never thought I was in sin, until I was taught the difference between mortal and venial sin. I knew then I might need some outside help getting into heaven. Mortal sin, I figured, I probably could avoid, but those venial sins were so easy to do without planning. Yelling at my mother came naturally to me, but I discovered it was a sin of not respecting my father and mother. Taking a piece of my sister's gum without permission was now a sin of stealing. Being late for church if through my own dawdling—oh yeah, check up another venial sin. Until I realized that I was getting pretty hard on myself, every week I had a long list of venial sins for confession on Friday.

When I was told I was "living in sin," I now knew what they meant. It took longer with venial sins, but those little sins collected like metal on a magnet, and I really needed confession and any other help, or I wasn't going to heaven, my nine-year-old mind told me.

When Sister told me what an indulgence was, I thought it was just what I needed. An indulgence, she said, was a partial or complete way of clearing your soul of all sin. In the 1500s, the wealthy could buy them, but lucky for us in the 1950s, they were free. They consisted of a certain prayer said a certain number of days and finished with a prayer of plenary indulgence, and all was wiped clean. Yep, no more sin until you started over.

Our Catechism (the book that taught us the practicing information of the Church) told us of seven outward signs of God's love that were given to us to help us gain grace. (Now it's getting complicated, I thought.) But, I understood, grace was the avenue to God, the presence of God in our lives, and the more we had, the closer to God we were living. The sacraments gave us that grace.

The first sacrament we received was Baptism. Our mother, father, and Catholic sponsors brought us just days after our birth to the baptismal font near or on the altar. I babysat many times for new moms in the neighborhood, and I would watch them, weak from childbirth, bringing their baby to church to prevent the possibility of the baby dying without baptism. When I asked what sins the baby had that baptism had to wipe away, I was told we all were born with an original sin from Adam and Eve. (It wasn't until we studied the Bible that I kind-of knew what that meant).

In the baptismal ceremony, the priest dropped water on the baby's forehead (probably washing away the sin, I thought), and the baby screeched with fear. The priest spoke Latin, but everyone looked like they knew what he was saying, or some would turn to their prayer books that translated Latin to English. At the end of the ceremony, the newly baptized baby, his very tired parents, his sponsors or godparents, the parents' family, and sometimes the priest would come to the baby's house for food (homemade, of course) and tea or coffee. The new mom would not only orchestrate the baptism ceremony with the priest but would also host the dinner party or small get-together to celebrate the acceptance of her baby into the Christian fold.

Exhaustion would settle in for everyone shortly after the guests left, except the baby; those newborns always seemed to realize their new life.

Our next sacrament, the Sacrament of Penance, demanded a lot from us small folks, but also really called upon the expertise and a little magic from those second-grade teachers. Those teachers were awesome! They accepted the ominous responsibility of changing wiggly, giggly, seven-year-olds into solemn penitents who would quietly close themselves into the pitch-black of the confessional and wait fearfully until the dark shadow appeared in the window above their heads. The clack of this window always startled me into the memorized response. "Bless me, Father, for I have sinned. This is my first confession. I have ..."(our list of sins would wait until we were having our First Confession, so we wouldn't use them in our practice confession). When I was finished and outside the confessional, almost every time I would realize there had been a word forgotten, or I had not finished my sin list—oh well.

Just as Penance was a private sacrament for the penitents, receiving the Holy Eucharist for the first time was a very public, family celebration in the cathedral. The organ and choir sang to our arrival as we climbed up the marble steps outside the church for our first Holy Communion. Well-dressed family and friends were waiting in the pews, and some took advantage of the moment by taking pictures of us with their Kodak Brownie cameras to memorialize our special day.

These homemade family photographers were bouncing in and out of the lines of their first communicants trying to get the best picture, while the sisters, who had worked so hard and long, making these seven-year-olds accept the solemnity and meaning of the day, looked upon their picture taking as not appropriate. We, however, would smile wide whenever we saw our family members.

Organ music again alerted our procession that the time had come. Our little bodies proudly clad in our First Communion dress moved forward in our well-rehearsed line. The color white was the common denominator for our clothing, and little individuality was allowed. The girls all wore white veils that fell to our shoulders or waists, but the head pieces were different, and our white dresses were also styled differently. We carried a rosary and a small, white prayer book. The boys wore white shirts, dress trousers with belts, and newly polished shoes. They held their hands in a prayerful stance, usually carrying dark, manly rosary beads.

We certainly felt special on this very special day, but it was more than our wonderful new clothes. The church itself seemed to have dressed up for our day. Candles twinkled and brightened the entire altar rail in anticipation of our arrival. White gladiolas spiked up from the huge bouquets of mums and carnations and greens on the altar The lights from the tiny spotlights placed high in the ceiling streamed their brightness down on our shoulders as the procession moved forward. Organ music set the step as we climbed into the first two pews, awaiting the others to assume their places at the altar.

The monsignor walked past the communion rail, up the marble stairs to the tall white altar, spoke that language again, and prepared the altar for the Mass and our First Holy Communion. Unlike the rehearsed sacrament of Penance, the teachers did not prepare us for the actual reception of the host.

After the moment had come and I was returning to my seat, no one knew the struggle that was going on in my mouth. I was not prepared for this tiny piece of unleavened bread, believed to be the Body of Christ, to grab the roof of my mouth and refuse to come off. Any tongue twisting, prodding, and pushing did no good, and the host remained cemented to the roof of my mouth as I nonverbally shared the struggle I was having with others entertaining the same fight. We knew we could not touch it, so dislodging it with our finger was not OK, and I just had to wait for it to dissolve and eventually release its hold on the roof of my mouth and fall onto my tongue. Fifteen minutes after receiving the Host and as Father was completing the Mass, I was finally able to say I had received my First Communion.

In researching this memoir, I found professional, in-studio photographs of both sides of my family dressed in First Communion suits or fancy dresses holding candles, prayer books, and rosaries, honoring their First Communion or some sacramental reception.

My First Communion and Confirmation pictures did not include a professional photographer studio stop, but our pictures show a wonderful, happy day, with lots of family, friends, gifts, wonderful mom-made food set out all day, and a cake (white, of course) with such good frosting. The joys of my day were preserved in the 3 x 3 dated photographs returned from film processing at Calandra Camera Store on 42nd and Dodge.

Sister told us that in our Baptism, our parents carried us to the baptismal font, answered for us the questions about our membership in Christ's community, and two Catholic adults witnessed the ceremony. When we received the sacraments of Penance and the Holy Eucharist, we were young Catholics, but Confirmation was different because we were now becoming adults in our faith. It was now our turn to accept the responsibility of the oncoming adulthood of our faith with a different ceremony and a new name, our confirmation name.

This seemed to be a more mature sacrament, I concluded. Unlike Baptism wherein our parents chose our name, we got to choose our confirmation name, usually a name of a saint whose life showed a good example. Rather than being carried up the aisle or walking in our new clothes with our prayer book and rosary, with this sacrament, we were all were in uniform white gowns with red collars, our hands folded in prayer. Mass, this time officiated by the bishop, moved slowly before we knelt at the communion rail to receive the sacrament of Confirmation.

It was like we were receiving the Eucharist, kneeling side by side at the communion railing, but this time it was different. The bishop, wearing his beautiful, celebratory dress, approached us, bent down so we could hand him the card that Sister had prepared for him that told him our new name, and he spoke English this time. His words said that God accepted us as adults in our faith, called me by the name I had chosen as my confirmation name—and then he lightly tapped our cheeks. I felt that slap all the way to my seat, even though it was slight. Sister had prepared us that the bishop would do this. She said it was to remind us that we must be strong in our faith in the trials of life. I didn't understand it then, but it soon became clear.

We did not receive the next sacrament for a long time, but we were experiencing it every day by living in our homes with parents working within their vow of marriage. Most of our parents had promised to live with and love one person of the opposite sex until death took one of them away. If they were living together intimately in any other form, they were considered living in sin: homosexual arrangements were mortal sin; heterosexual couples not married in the Catholic church were also living a life of sin. The couple that was divorced was bound by their vow and could not marry again.

A courthouse divorce was a civil activity and had no bearing upon their initial blessed vow in the eyes of the church.

It was difficult being divorced in the 1950s Catholic Church .The adults in a divorce (you could never say Catholic divorce because there was no such thing), were sometimes treated as a threat to the marriages that did exist, and divorcees many times were ostracized from social activities within the church. Sacraments were denied to the divorcee. If they were dating or had a serious relationship, in the Church's eyes you were still married, so you were violating your vows. Divorced women with children were considered failures, and divorced men with children were considered brave for assuming the responsibility that was his.

Marriage vows trumped all: physical and sexual abuse, any neglect or control issues, fiscal misuse, substance abuse, abuse of children, or sexual or emotional infidelity. When the church looked at marriage in this decade, you were simply counseled that you should make it work, and it was usually the woman to whom that directive was made.

Some divorced men or women would seek an absolution to the marriage vow but found it difficult. There was an administrative board in most dioceses, established for this purpose, and they reviewed all verification of abuse, abandonment, or whatever caused the break-up of this marriage. This board requested dates, places, and witness information on the many sheets to be filled out. It was very detailed and difficult for many to relive, so many cases were just dropped. Another reason cases were discontinued was the cost. It was a very expensive commitment for many, and if the cost could not be met, the board would refuse to review the case.

Children in a divorced family also found life more difficult in the church and school. My friend, whose mom had escaped from an abusive marriage, would roll her eyes when she was called from class to the office and would mumble, "Here we go again." Her uniform was too short, blouse too tight, or they were always checking under her neck scarf for hickies, and she shouldn't dye her hair—the list went on. Because of these complaints, I began noticing the treatment she was receiving as different from mine and ascribed it only to the fact she lived with her divorced mother, while my family arrangement was more of a traditional Catholic family.

The other vow that lasted a lifetime in the 1950s was that of Holy Orders or the vow a priest took after years of preparation in a seminary. "Once a priest, always a priest" is what we were told, and their preparation to priesthood guided them to this commitment. A boy suspecting "his calling to the priesthood" was nurtured and guided by priests, sisters, and community. Boys many times were encouraged to leave their co-ed high school and attend a boys-only seminary high school during their teen years, but many chose to attend the seminary after graduation from their high school. Whichever path the future priest chose, they were a very special young man in the eyes of their families, neighborhood, and church.

When the graduation from their formal seminary education brought them into parish, cloistered, or mission work, the bishop exposed these young men to a variety of experiences before their final vows. The church wanted the future priest to be aware of the services and temptations they would face as a priest and realize the importance and permanence of their vow. Cathedral had always been known for presenting a variety of experiences within the parish structure. St. Cecilia's Cathedral had two major hospitals in its parameter; maintained a high school and an elementary school; serviced professional, wealthy parish members and very poor parish members (all attending the Cathedral schools with no formal tuition); developed outstanding fund raising opportunities; and of course hosted all the Catholic celebratory traditions of the bishop. A lucky, young priest assigned to Cathedral received exposure to all elements of parish life and was usually seen in his later priestly life as a monsignor or bishop.

Girls considering becoming a sister were also nurtured by the religious and community. Our sisters, the Sinsinawa Dominicans, would sense that a girl was interested in becoming a religious sister, and they would begin giving information in pamphlets, retreat opportunities, visitations to their home, and even invitations to the mother house in Sinsinawa, Wisconsin. Formal education to the sisterhood, however, usually began after high school graduation. Toward the end of their senior year, interested girls would visit different mother houses for a face-to-face visit of the community of their choice.

Each community had a different service as their primary vision. I was most aware of the Dominican sisters who taught all ages and all genders of children and the madams (now called sisters) of the Sacred Heart whose all-girls' schools educated women from elementary through university level. There were many other orders, which allowed women to follow "their calling" and do God's work. Most Catholic schools were manned with sisters and a few lay teachers; most Catholic hospitals were manned by medically trained sisters and a few lay nurses; food banks, orphanages, counseling centers, and shelters were usually staffed with well-educated nuns who were social workers. Both administrators and workers were wonderfully cheap labor for their Catholic services during this time.

Other choices were missionary clergy, working to meet the needs of the very poor in primitive nations. Their work was made more visible to teenagers when these missionaries returned to the US to raise money for their poor villages. They not only raised our awareness of their work, but we also met the poor we did not know existed in the world. They spoke to the entire parish during all Masses and sometimes visited our school classes. Pictures of barefoot moms and scantily clad children with swollen bellies embellished their stories and brought dollars easily out of the pockets of almost everyone in attendance.

The last sacrament we only learned about when one of our family members had died in our presence. This was Extreme Unction. In the 1950s, this sacrament was usually given only once and was between the priest and the person dying. It involved a "last confession," so the dying person and the priest were alone. When the dying person received absolution, their body was anointed with oils, which gave family members and the person receiving this sacrament a sense of peace and readiness for death.

Mary

Looking down the aisle of a '50s classroom, one would find an interesting commonality. Almost every girl sitting in those wooden desks would have the name *Mary* intertwined somehow in their name. Upon introduction, you would meet Mary Ann, Mary Fran, Mary Jo, Mary Lou. Mary Joan, Mary Ellen, Mary Jean, Mary Cecilia, Mary Pat, Mary Agnes, Marietta. Maria, if Mary was not in our first names, it was probably a second name or confirmation name, such as Margaret Mary, Jean Marie, and Patricia Mary. Even the names chosen by our sister-teachers included "Mary": Sister Mary Constantine, Sister Mary Mineve, Sister Mary Viola, Sister Mary Lamberta, Sister Mary Adrian, Sister Mary Perrine. (This was your great aunt Bertie's name when she was a Dominican sister.)

Naming me "Mary Ellen" came from my mother's strong belief in the Blessed Mother and a bargain my mother made with her. My mother summed it up this way: "Your father wanted our first child to be a boy, and I wanted a girl, so I prayed to Mary for help. My prayers promised that if she gave us a girl, I would name that girl Mary, and I would pin a Miraculous Medal of Mary on your (my) diaper." When I appeared female, she kept that promise; that tiny medal, which graced my diaper until I was potty trained, is dangling from a gold bracelet today, and I was named Mary Ellen in honor of Mary and my Irish grandmother Ellen.

My mother would not accept the possibility that some sociologists have proclaimed, saying that Mary was a myth or just a goddess story. Mary was Mom's "go-to" for any intention and a guide through difficult times of her life. Lillian Mary (my mom) never agreed with non-Catholic friends that Catholics almost made a God out of Mary with all the dedicated church chapels, all the prayer cards dedicated to her, or the many statues they saw in any Catholic church, home, or yard. Lill never had any doubt about her guide, the "Mother of God."

Usually very frugal, my mother never questioned when one year, I wanted to use the majority of my birthday money to buy a plaster statue of Mary for the room Bert and I shared. Mom took me on the Dodge Street bus down to Cosgraves Religious Store for my purchase. When my stash didn't provide enough money for my choice of statues, Mom supplemented the rest. Our statue stood proudly between Bert's and my beds until our lives changed, and we no longer shared a bedroom.

Other Mary stories from our family also surfaced. My favorite came from my Czech great-grandmother. We are a close family, and we had our Nonie until I was twenty-three. She loved to tell stories of early Omaha, her trip to the United States, and of course, her family stories. Her Mary story involved her trip to the US. She reported how the family had saved their coins for passage for her younger sister and her to make the trip to the United States with the plan of getting jobs and then bringing the rest of the family over.

They were to leave from Lisbon, Portugal, in the belly of a small steamship. Passage purchased, the girls traveled from their Czech home to Lisbon, but found when they had arrived that the ship had already set sail. They were despondent, until they learned, some months later, that the ship had gone down in a storm, and not one passenger or crew member had been saved!

This did not stop them from saving for the next trip, however. When the needed amount was collected for their second passage from Lisbon, one of their family members brought a package for them to take on this voyage. When the blanket was unwrapped, they saw the statue of a wooden Black Madonna holding the Infant of Prague. Keeping with the Eastern European Black Madonna story, they had included clothes to put on the statue at different seasons. My Noni and her sister kept the statue near them in the bowels of the ship like a modern St. Christopher medal, patron of travel. This crossing of the Atlantic and across the land to Omaha, Nebraska, was successful. The Black Madonna was passed on to me!

Recently I took this Black Madonna and my story to a TV program called *Antiques Roadshow*. The antique expert listened carefully to my story, and when he attempted to set a value on it, he stated that a 175 year old, hand-carved wooden statue of Mary and her Son had very little value in the antique world, but in our family, its value probably could not be measured. He could not be more correct. This Black Madonna statue now stands on the landing, leading to our upstairs looking down over the family life below. I am reminded of the pain and hardships faced by the women before me and say a prayer of gratitude for the strength and faith they displayed.

The story of Mary's life has always been entangled in tradition and interpretation, and there are many traditional beliefs about her that I question. I don't think Mary ascended bodily into heaven. Mary's virgin birth of Jesus, I don't care. I always thought tradition and male interpretation had built her story. It has never been fiction or myth to me, simply a guiding presence.

For example, later in my life when one of my children was in the throes of a powerful illness, and depression brought him to the lowest levels, I wrote this poem as I watched him in the struggle of mental illness.

Mary, melting down the cross of your Son,
Tears streaming, limbs numbing, breath
refusing to come.
Looking at your own: tortured, suf-
fering, and rent,
Not knowing and wondering, why was
this sent?

Beyond your misery, you send me comfort
in your cry,
As you teach me to bear up,
And in my pain, ask why.

WIDENING OUR VIEW

During the Lenten season of every elementary school year, a stack of flattened boxes would always appear on Sister's desk. Pictures of children would appear as we matched the top and sides forming our boxes. Sister would explain that these were just some of the children around the world, who were starving and needed our support. Each Friday, we were to bring coins that we were to save throughout the week and collect in our boxes. She told her attentive audience that we had a chance to help the starving children of the world by adopting a baby with this money. Needless to say, all of us would clean out our mom and dad's pockets or tap our allowance funds to put the jingle in our box.

When our pennies, dimes, or whatever we brought totaled $10.00, Sister would donate our monies to the Holy Childhood Society; she would give us a certificate of adoption, and we could name our baby. One year, I named my baby my teacher's name, and when I told her what I had named my baby, I watched tears begin to pool in her eyes. She kept her composure as she led us down the stairs to recess, but I saw the tears running down her shiny cheeks as we reached the bottom of the stairs. Only she and I knew why they were wet; but I didn't think it would make her sad.

Although the coins in our boxes gave support for hungry children and the Holy Childhood Society awakened us to others' needs, I remember having questions. What would happen to my baby when it ate through the $10.00? Did its parents care if I renamed their baby? How expensive are groceries there? Would the Holy Childhood Society just re-adopt babies when they had eaten up the $10.00? No one ever answered my questions.

May was a special month at St. Cecilia's; not only was the school year coming to a close, but Sister called it "Mary's month." One morning, there was something different in our classroom, and Sister was smiling more than usual. In the front corner of the room stood a statue of Mary on boxes covered in blue construction paper, Mary's color.

Sister told us that she had built our May altar over the weekend, and now it was time for our part in the project. We were to make it beautiful for Mary by bringing flowers from home to surround her. The flowers began to appear. It was such a delight to walk into our May classroom: floral smells filled the room, and new colors brightened a normally dull corner. "We were such good flower collectors," Sister proudly told us, "I had to borrow vases from some of the other teachers."

Then one morning, Sister walked in with a sad face followed by the principal. We knew this was serious, as the principal seldom visited our classroom, and we exchanged puzzled looks as we stood in respect for her arrival. Sister started her admonition; it had come to the attention of her office that in our innocence and desire to honor Mary, we may have been guilty of stealing. The neighbors had been reporting that on our route to school, we were picking their newly planted flowers and bringing them to our altar. Those neighbors were not happy, and neither was Sister Principal. Our flower supply fell drastically, and the room returned to its original decor except for Mary standing on her blue altar with a few blossoms around her.

GIRL SCOUT REJECT

Outside of the elementary classroom, our parents were always broadening our talents by exposing us to new experiences. When the note came home that my friend Jeanie's mother was starting a Brownie troupe and had invited me to join, I gladly accepted. Mom ordered my brown uniform and hat from Brandeis Department Store. After school on Thursday, all of the young Girl Scouts, called Brownies, skipped and ran down the hill to the corner house for our meeting. We did crafts, we cooked, and we slept over; it was a great time. Our leader worked hard to make it fun and educational. At one meeting, we were told of a Girl

Scout project that we were to be a part of; we were to sell Girl Scout cookies just like the older girls!

When they handed out the paperwork for our cookie selling, I put them in my homework folder, so I wouldn't lose them. This was special. On my way home, I thought, "Why don't I use this time and take orders as I head home?"—and that's what I did. All of our neighbors were so glad to see that Girl Scout cookies were back, and I was excited with the number of orders I had solicited just walking home. I knew our Brownie leader would be pleased.

However, she was not. In my excitement, I evidently had not heard that the sale began next Monday, and the mothers of my fellow Brownies were very angry that I had "canvassed" the parish and had quite a list of sales before their daughters had a chance to sell their cookies. The local Girl Scout board met, listened to the angry mothers, and reviewed my transgression. Their decision was that I was not to go back to Brownies; I had been kicked out of the Brownies!

For the irony of this story, you must fast forward some forty years to a large Victorian home in Tarkio, Missouri. We purchased this wonderful, three-story, brick home with its wrap-around porch, ten-foot ceilings, a parlor, living room, formal dining room, kitchen, foyer and two pantries on the first floor. Such a home!

One night shortly after we moved in, I received a phone call with a request. The Girl Scouts in Tarkio, the county seat of Atchison County, had cookies coming for the North East Missouri cookie sales, but they had no storage area for the weekend. The cookies were coming, and they needed a large place to store them just for the weekend. They asked if there was any way that we could store them in our home and promised that the leaders and scouts would come and pick them up on Monday. We agreed, and Friday the semi-truck backed up to our wrap-around front porch to begin unloading what seemed to be endless boxes of cookies. When the porch could not take more boxes, the men filled the parlor, then the living room, then the dining room, and next the foyer; large rooms all.

Boxes were stacked from the floor to the ten-foot ceilings in all rooms with only a person-wide path guiding us through the labyrinth to the bathroom or other necessary doors. As promised on Monday morning, the leaders and Scouts began collecting the cookies from our home. In appreciation for the Olssons saving the day, I, the Brownie reject of 1951, was proclaimed "Honorary Girl Scout Cookie Chairman of Atchison County" in 1983.

THE JOHNSON SISTERS

My sister and I both wanted to take piano lessons, and there were two sisters who conveniently taught in their house down the hill from the church. One sister taught Bert piano lessons upstairs, and the other sister taught me art downstairs. Art for me was so much fun, and Bert's desired piano lessons became work, hard work—with homework to the point that, after a few months, she asked to come downstairs and play at art with me. My mom being an artist herself agreed, of course, and the two of us went to our lessons in the basement together. These ladies gave us both skills that enhanced our whole lives.

Occasionally to keep us interested in our lessons, Mom would give us a dime. After our lessons, we could stop at the local grocery store on 40th and California Streets and buy a package of Hostess cupcakes or Twinkies, or we could stop at the tiny Reed's ice cream store and buy an ice cream cone, whose ice cream was cut from a tube of your chosen flavor and placed in the top of the cone.

The Johnson sisters did not have railings on their front stairway, and one day Bert fell off the side of the steps, and her eye tooth went straight through her upper lip. She cried for a while, but my promises of an ice cream cone quieted her. We purchased the ice cream at the Reeds Ice Cream stand, and the cold must have numbed the pain because Bert was blowing bloody, ice cream bubbles through the hole in her lip before we got home.

WHEE! BIKE FUN

My horizons and independence enlarged as my means of transportation changed. As I outgrew my Radio Flyer Wagon and moved to my skates and scooter, my playground grew from my yard and alley to my neighborhood. Few cars on side streets allowed longer street play during the day and evening.

One of my favorite rides in our neighborhood was pushing my scooter through the neighborhood, with one leg pushing and the other riding on the two-wheeled machine. I loved the speed. Other neighbor kids joined me, and in our minds we resembled a herd of mustangs galloping up the hills and flying down with our manes flowing in the wind. Our herd of scooter-mustangs changed, however, when bikes replaced our scooters, bringing real speed to our fun.

Some of the group had new Schwinn bikes, but most of us had second-hand bikes that worked just fine. My bike was a cast-off bike from my aunt who had outgrown biking (which I never did). It was too big for my stubby legs and had big, red balloon tires. I was a sight, but what a wonderful machine! It opened worlds of fun for me.

Almost every night after dinner and homework, Elmer (my dog) and I would head out for a run. Elmer was a short-legged dog, but those little legs would keep up with me and my bike at any speed. This nightly ritual was a welcome break from all the sitting still and silence during my day at school. Our usual path was racing north on 44th, pulling hard on my pedals up the Cass Street hill, and then letting gravity have its way with me and my bike down the steep Wakeley hill. Our jaunt would cover our neighborhood streets until the lighting of the street lights would stop the fun. We were ready to come home though; Elmer and I were always a tuckered twosome.

In junior high when I found my friend, Char, who also loved cycling, we left our neighborhood streets and rode to Elmwood Park in west Omaha. On any Saturday morning, Char and I would be biking west down Dodge Street with the lunches we had packed the night before bouncing in the baskets on the front of our bikes. We respected the red lights and traffic as we wormed our way to the natural woodland that surrounded the neatly manicured golf course. We would ride past the tidy greens and the lonesome playground equipment, and park our bikes just outside the inviting woods.

The low-hanging limbs of the old deciduous trees, surrounding bushes, and upstart seedlings slapped our sweaty bodies as we entered their embrace. After a short struggle through their standing defense, we found the purpose and the treasure in our trip, the stream that slowly wound through the park. Until hunger stopped our work, we built log bridges, stick dams, and followed the footprint paths of creatures that had walked through the sand and mud, and we laughed and giggled as we worked. Although our preadolescent minds didn't know John Muir's quote, "In every walk with nature, one receives more than he seeks," we realized it every time we rode our bikes westward and entered that secret garden.

Lunch call was the growling of our tummies, and we retreated to civilization and our bag lunches waiting in the baskets of our bikes. Sunlight made us squint as we climbed onto the manmade picnic tables near the carefully designed golf course. Bologna sandwiches, Hostess cupcakes, and our apples never tasted so good. When lunch was finished, a short sit on the benches, a few swings on the playground equipment seeing who could go the highest, and we were a tired twosome heading east on Dodge Street to our homes, savoring our day.

TECHNICOLOR PLEASURES

Going to the movies on the weekends became an important daytime activity. Both the Admiral Theater and the Dundee Theater were within walking distance of our home, and my sister and I loved begging a dollar from our parents for a movie, a drink, and popcorn. Both theaters showed a variety of movies, and we loved being whisked away in a Pat Boone musical or a Debbie Reynolds love story. But censure again moved in, and we learned not all movies were good for us.

We were taught that there were good movies and bad movies. In fact, it was a mortal sin if you went to a "B" movie or, God forbid, an "X" movie, so you wanted to make sure you checked the church listings in the Catholic newspaper, the *True Voice*. One time I had not checked that list when I went to a movie with a public school friend, and later I discovered that it was a "B" movie that we saw. I was horrified that I was in sin. It walked through my thoughts constantly; until, ah, at last, Friday confession.

That Friday I welcomed a sacrament that I had never felt very valuable. This time I needed forgiveness, but I feared the response Father would give to *mortal sin*, so I chose very carefully the priest known for his small penances (the task you had to do to make amends for your sin) and kind words. The line was long outside his confessional as usual, and I don't think any line has ever moved as slowly. In my wait, I mentally rehearsed the way I would break it to Father that I was in mortal sin and damned to hell. I decided to simply follow the form I was taught with the hope Father would not notice such a serious sin.

Finally, it was my turn to enter the dark confessional and wait for that familiar sound of the wood hitting wood as the window opened. Again the wait. The silence and the dark was like a petri dish for my guilt. Wack—and there he was behind the curtain. I swallowed hard, dryness stopping my words.

"Are you there?" he asked, and I finally pushed out my first words. I whispered ever so quietly the usual, "Bless me Father ..." and when I came to my list of sins, I had buried my mortal one in the middle of venial sins, praying he would not hear it. "*You did what*?" he shouted when he heard my buried sin. My mind went directly to the long line of students outside Father's confessional who now knew the next person to leave this confessional door had sinned grievously.

"Father, ah, it, ah was, ah, an accident, er ..." I tried to say, but the usually kind Father interrupted.

"Did you enjoy it?" he asked with less volume.

"It was a good story," I answered innocently.

He hollered again, "Do you realize how wrong that is?"

I nodded thinking he could see me in the dark, but his words continued stressing how badly I had acted, and how I must promise God that I would check the *True Voice* for the listing before I went to the movies again. I nodded again and crept out of the confessional, eyes down and a hefty penance to complete. You can be sure that I checked the *True Voice* every time after that.

PLAYLAND PARK

As the tulips poked their heads out of the newly thawed ground each spring and young folks were able to burst outside to play into the warm air, the Catholic school student not only looked forward to the end of the school year approaching, but another traditional event trumpeted summer's coming. The Playland Amusement Park, just across the bridge in Council Bluffs, Iowa, sent all Catholic grade schools discount coupons each year for Ascension Thursday.

We were off school for this Holy Day, and our parents gladly took advantage of the bargain and gave us enough money for rides at the Park and for the bus ride crossing the bridge to Playland. Bert, my friend Rita, and I had other plans; we would not buy the transfer to the bus that crossed the river. Instead, we would walk over the bridge to the Park, saving the 25 cents for more rides. It was such a fun day every year.

Our young stomachs usually tolerated the spinning, rolling, and being tossed from one fear to another. We paid the duck-tailed workers to continue our torture as we moved ride to ride, loving it all. On one ride, however, my friend vomited her undigested pink cotton candy, and hot dog into my lap as the Octopus twirled us. I remember both of us washing up in the restroom and continuing on with our day.

One could always tell the next day who had gone to the Park. With wind whipped hair, red faces and arms, and lingering smiles, we tried to stay awake and struggle to give Sister our attention.

Friends Forever?

Most of our class had been together since first grade, some even from kindergarten, and by junior high, the friendships had solidified into cliques. Sometimes groups developed from neighborhoods (walking home), sometimes families (cousins), and sometimes money. But over the years, being in the same class with the same people, our friendships became somewhat permanent and exclusive. It was when these friendships became cruel to those outside these groups, the sisters entered the picture. Subtle bullying developed easily and in response, sermons would erupt from Sister, preaching the Christian way of life. Sadly, it often fell on deaf ears of many of us. Then it was Father's turn to stress the unchristian way we were treating each other, and he too was seldom successful.

Every student, Catholic or public school, has their story of hurt during this time of life. It could be severe criticism for being different as bodies developed early, erupting acne, jealousy, weight, and each story pulling up pain. Some of the targets in our class were, a very bright girl who wore unpopular shoes, another who was an accomplished toe ballerina, someone slow to shave their legs, another whose chest bounced before the rest of us and, of course, the fat boy or girl who could not run bases—all innocent targets of the group. Whatever the issue, research is showing that the damage is painful and lasting.

My story involves a friend who became so close that she would invite me to her family farm. I collected eggs, walked beans, irrigated corn fields with pipes, drove a truck at thirteen, cared for a calf, yes a calf. Oh, I thought I was in heaven year after year. Her family was my family. I was a city kid who was working out in nature with my friend and loving every minute. I'm not even sure what caused my being ejected from our group of friends at school, but it included rejection from her family as well. Losing my skating buddy was another part of in this loss. Becoming an isolate was painful, but missing my friends was the true pain.

With the exit of some students at the end of eighth grade and an influx of students from all over Omaha in the ninth grade, our social dynamics had changed, however. New, exciting people were allowed into cliques that had excluded others over the years, and some people left membership in the existing groups and joined other groups. For girls, the appearance of new boys also changed who was friends with whom. These new folks seemed to stir the pot of our traditional friend dynamics, and we loved it.

SOMETHINGS OLD,
SOMETHINGS NEW

Graduation from eighth grade at St. Cecilia's was an event to remember, especially for the girls. The sisters made it a party for these budding teenagers. The girls celebrated being out of uniform (hurrah) with new outfits, nylon socks, and shoes, and sometimes bound in by their first panty girdles. All of the girls were given a flower to carry, and the boys, dressed in their best church clothes, simply folded their hands together as we processed up the long aisle.

Mrs. F. would set our marching pace with the tempo of the music she had chosen. We kept our eyes straight ahead, trying not to look at our large Catholic families proudly watching us graduate from eighth grade. Girls would wobble down the aisle on their first one- or two-inch heels, sporting knee-high panty hose, all new facets to our eighth-grade wardrobes. But in this procession, unlike the bishop's processions, we would walk pass the first five lines of empty pews and up the white marble stairs to the altar to form our rehearsed formations.

I concluded that this must be a very special time because I had never seen girls on the altar; never saw a girl priest; never saw a girl help the priest in Mass; never saw a girl lead the singing from the altar. Even when we wore our long white dresses in the bishop's processions, girls went into the first two pews before we reached the altar. Yet that day, there we were , boys *and* girls on the altar, awaiting our eighth-grade graduation certificates from Father. Being on the altar was nothing new for the boys; they had been altar boys since fifth grade, and assistants during the bishop's processions for most of their elementary years. The boys did not realize how really special this day was for us girls.

Moving to the high school, however, was not all new. The elementary building had always shared the high school cafeteria for lunches, so we were familiar with the basement kitchen and its enticing smells that wafted down the tunnel under the street and up into elementary hallways, calling us to lunch. The elementary students always ate first, and only Sister's presence changed our hunger-driven run in the tunnel to a civilized walk to the food at its end. As we neared the sounds of the cafeteria, there was a constant roar from aluminum chairs and tables screaming annoyance of being disturbed, and loud student voices rejoicing in their fresh release from three hours of near silence.

Although we were familiar with the cafeteria, the high school building itself had always been blond-bricked mystery, sitting silently across the street with happenings that we didn't understand. We had watched our older brothers, sisters, and neighbors come and go, wearing uniforms different from ours, and we watched them standing around talking and laughing in boy-and-girl groups. Some of the students from other parishes were old enough to drive their own cars and even smoke cigarettes (not allowed on school property), so we watched the smokers duck below the dashboard to light their Marlboros or Winstons as they sped out of the parking lot. This all was a mystery to us, but we knew we were about to be one of them. Our formal, eighth-grade graduation had pushed us out of the nest and across the street to a new world.

Little did we know the changes we would experience within those brick walls. No longer did we walk in silent lines to the lavatory or the next class; we could talk and laugh in the hallways and cafeteria. No longer did we visit the bathrooms at Sister's discretion or schedule, we were allowed to leave our class with our pass and urinate as our bodies reported the need. We no longer read from tiny classroom libraries; our school library now seemed huge and included works that spoke adult stuff. We no longer sat all day in the same desk, changing subjects only by the book called for by Sister, and we now walked to our next subject after our preparatory dash to our locker for the correct book. No longer did we house our books and supplies in an 8 x 11 box attached under our desktop; all of our needs—our texts, notebooks, coats, and hats were crammed into one of the assigned lockers lining the hallways. There were no cloak rooms in this new world.

BLACKBURN'S AND WILLY'S
PHARMACIES

And then there was Blackburn's. As grade school students, we knew about the fun that went on after school at Blackburn's Drug on Cummings Street. We also knew we had to be high school students before we could hang out there. But we had crossed the street; we were high school students now and were ready for being a part of that Blackburn world.

This local drugstore was the hub of Cathedral High students' after-school social life. Romances had blossomed, flourished, and ended in the booths of its soda fountain. The brightly colored nuke box set the beat of the room as bobby socks and penny loafer shoes moved to its sounds, and friendships grew.

It had that drugstore smell, and colored crepe paper fans decorated the windows, advertising Cokes, root beer, sundaes, malts, and a few food items for the hungry teenage bodies that flooded in every afternoon.

And now our turn had come; we were of age, er, so we thought. We were dismayed at our first student body meeting when they announced that Blackburns was off limits to the entire Cathedral student body this year. The moan from the crowd was palpable.

"But why?" we asked.

It was reported that complaints from the other patrons of the store brought them to this decision. It was told to us that a detention (one hour after school) would be given to anyone breaking this rule. The administration and Blackburns didn't realize they were tampering with tradition for the older students and a strong desire for the younger students, and the threat of a detention didn't stop much of the traffic to the much-loved store. So the next edict was "expulsion from school" as their final attempt to stop the flow of students into their favorite haunt after school, and expulsion scared everyone. Bingo, we did not go after that.

There was another drugstore nearby, but their soda fountain wasn't as appealing; no dance floor, and no jute box, just drinks and various ice cream treats served to you by the "soda jerk" as you sat on tall stools in front of the high fountain bar. It was clear this soda fountain was set up for business, not the social life Blackburns invited.

Be Bop A Loo La

The Kauths loved music, and we loved to dance. Our parents met, dancing on roller skates as late teens. The whole family square danced for years, and my father taught me how to ballroom dance (only after a few beers).

Our mother had her radio, singing to us from morning to dinner time. Her favorite stations were KOIL and PBS (or its startup), so we were exposed to some classical music, modern 1950 music, as well as our father's preferences of Nat King Cole, Perez Prado, the Sons of the Pioneers, Bing Crosby, Dean Martin, and Glenn Miller. Whew, such a variety of music, but even more artists and music genre joined the mix when Bert and I introduced Rock and Roll to the collection with our 45 rpms.

We played and danced downstairs in our dad-built recreation room to so many different artists: Bill Haley and the Comets, Pat Boone, Little Anthony and the Imperials, Johnny Mathias, The Lime lighters, Connie Stevens, The Everly Brothers, the Drifters, just to name a few. Music was a welcome companion in our home and our trips in the car.

In early spring, the windows of our home would be opened, and the cocktail of fresh, cool breezes and music from the record player would celebrate the coming of the new season. Days like that would fill all of our senses. So when I learned the school had dances in the cafeteria for all of the high school classes, even freshmen, I could not wait. One thing I could not imagine, however, was what they would do to make the cafeteria fun.

CAFETERIA DANCES

Even in high school, the hungry teenage bodies ran down the stairs at the lunch bell and waited impatiently outside the windowless, fluorescent-lit room to eat what they had been smelling for the last hours. Now we were going to party in that same room? When our first dance night came, and we finally walked down the gym steps, we were surprised to see the metamorphosis behind those doors.

The cafeteria had lost all of its usual aura. All distinguishable signs of food service were gone, and the enticing smells were no longer advertising food. The usual din of furniture and students had quieted and were replaced with melodies and soft talk. Crepe paper was stretched over the florescent lights in an attempt to romanticize the dance floor and produce a mellow yellow, blue, or red world.

There was still one problem that stretched crepe paper and romantic sounds could not change. Most dancers at the Cathedral dances were the same people we sat next to in class each day, and now we were to dance with these same people in the same room in which we ate lunch. For a while, the "same old" fizzled away a lot of spontaneity, but as record after record dropped from the stack on the 45 rpm record player, more and more joined the rhythm of the dance floor, and we were able to enjoy each other on a different level.

Favorite songs and heart-throb artists would play with our overstimulated emotions and sometimes even draw the boys from one wall to invite the girls on the other wall to dance. Those girls not invited to dance enjoyed girl talk and girl-to-girl fast dances throughout the night, and even they called it a fun dance.

When the tempo of the music quickened, everyone would rush to the dance floor, boys and girls and girls with girls jitterbugging to "Rockin' Robin," or hopping to "At the Hop" or some other fast-paced music blaring from the record player. Polka music, or dances like the calypso, the mash, or the stroll kept those who knew the correct steps on the dance floor, or brave boys who had received a quick tutorial by some girl. There was some unwritten rule that said a girl must be chosen by a boy when the tempo slowed, so the dance floor would empty and slowly repopulate when a crooner began singing their love songs.

DRIVE-TO DANCES

If you had a vehicle or a friend with a car, you could always find a dance on the weekend at some gym (usually a Catholic school gym for us) with low lights and good music ready to guide our bodies into motion. Holy Angel dances in North Omaha never produced a boyfriend or even a date for me, but it was such a good time! When the Holy Angel Church announced an upcoming dance, students from all over Omaha would drive the distance, dance all night, and groan when the last dance was announced. Gals like me, who came with girl friends, would leave laughing and perhaps with the hope that "he" might call.

Cathedral, unlike Holy Angels, seldom had dances in their gym for fear of damaging the shiny wooden floor. When they did allow us to dance on it, they made us remove our shoes (hence the term "sock hop"). Cafeteria dances must have just been easier: easier to decorate and easier to control the dancers and the kinds of music and attire (there were rules then too).

WHAT TO WEAR, WHAT TO WEAR

There always seemed to be rules as to what we could wear. Our uniforms, of course, kept everything appropriate during the school day, but when we were out of uniform, other rules of dress fell into place.

It was not uncommon for dance attendees to be sent home if the chaperoning sisters and priests deemed their attire inappropriate. Girls could not wear low-cut blouses or sweaters that hugged their chests too tightly. Boys still could not wear jeans or tight trousers as the popular style dictated. Girls' dresses (especially at prom) had to be no more than one thumb length from the base of your throat and had to cover your shoulders. Strapless gowns, so popular in public high schools and movies, were taboo at our dances. The length of prom dresses were either long (ankle length) or short (mid-calf) length.

Costume accessories also received scrutiny. Heavy makeup, tattoos, exchanged class rings dangling from your neck or bulging with wound yarn on your finger, and ear piercing was looked down upon as classless, and sometimes the student was asked to correct their image or not return. Fingernail polish or nylon stockings were accepted for dances, but not for daily wear. Even girls' patent leather shoes were discouraged. (The word had it there was a fear that the boys could look up our skirts.)

Hair styles were left alone for the most part, except for the boy who needed a haircut, had used too much Brylcreme, or had trained a "duck tail" into their hair style. These styles spoke "rowdy" and were not considered appropriate for Catholic school students. What seems to be silly limits to our clothing now were accepted then and seen as tickets into our desired dance or activity.

When we were out of uniform, we just stepped into a different uniform. Guys wore letter sweaters, t-shirts, sweaters, or sports shirts. Their blue or khaki pants had no pleats and sometimes sported a buckled insert on the back of the trouser at the top of the buttocks (not allowed in school because they scratched the desks). Their clothing looked new, and the boys smelled better too, usually of Old Spice or a nice-smelling soap. Their shoes were usually slip on style, sometimes with buckles, ties, or a slot for pennies. Their new uniform was not as drastic a change as the girls' when we were out of our green vests and skirts.

There was such a sense of freedom when a girl could cast off her usual school uniform and don her new look. Our daily relaxed hair styles became a teased and sprayed frame around a face more heavily made up with Maybelline cosmetics, and many of us smelled of "Evening in Paris." Our jewelry was usually a colored plastic complement to our outfit, like pop-it-beads that pulled apart and made necklaces or bracelets depending upon its length. Skirts were mid-calf length, and full skirts were held out by layers and layers of crinoline petticoats. A jitterbug twist or twirl would send our crinoline skirts into full exposure. Some girls wore straight skirts with matching sweaters and the cardigan of the set simply covered the shoulders and was held in position with a chain that had a decorative clamp on either end. If there was no cardigan, many times the sweater had a fake collar under it that was usually crocheted or embroidered. "Sister or Father Guard" at the door governed our attire and makeup. Even these nights of freedom had their rules.

During the school day, some girls pulled their cotton bobby socks up their leg and rolled them down into a large bundle around the ankle. To make the roll even larger, we placed a cut-off cuff from another sock at the top of the sock, and rolled it down, forming an even more gigantic bundle around the ankle.

This look was to supposedly make our ankles look smaller, but walking with a swag became a problem, and this fad was short lived. At the dances, however, we wore ballerina slip-on shoes or our dress shoes with knee high nylons or stockings. Shoe rules relaxed as the '50s went on, and Baker's and Kinney's Shoes became the place to shop, except for my parents.

AHHH, PEONY PARK

Peony Park caused many wonderful memories for most students in the 1950s. It was a sizeable plot of land just outside the Omaha city limits. It had been developed for family fun, and the white youth of Omaha could enjoy every facet of the park. It was much better than a simple park; it had a large, lake-like swimming pool with diving docks and boards, twelve-foot bubbling fountains, picnic areas, hiking and bike trails, an outside band stand, and an inside ball room, all plunked into the center of a natural wonderland of trees, paths, and bushes.

It was a joy for us throughout the year. In the summer, my cousin, Ellen, and I taught swimming there, and my sister and I spent many summer days swimming in the big swimming lake with its splashing, noisy fountains and floating docks. In the fall and winter months, schools and organizations had dances at the outside bandstand or inside ballroom. For proms, homecoming dances, and fundraisers, we danced to local bands: the Eddy Haddad Orchestra, Johnny Ray Gomez Band, and sometimes even famous traveling orchestras.

The sounds and smells of each season differed in Peony Park, but throughout the park, there was an aura so different and so much more magical than our cafeteria and gym dances. One was easily whisked away into that wonderland. The far-away smacking sounds of the water falling down the five-tiered water fountains strategically placed around the pool would welcome you as you left your car and moved toward the dance pavilion. Moving down the path amid the greenery, we would detect flora of all types: fragrant hydrangeas, petunias, lilies, and lilacs. Huge multicolored leaves leaned occasionally into the path of the arriving dancers. The carefully manicured grounds, fragrant flowers, and the glistening pool reflected the blinking white lights that turned the evening into an surreal, magical world even before we reached the dance floor.

Everyone was almost unrecognizable to each other at first, wearing our formals and sport coats and sporting boutonnieres and corsages (usually fragrant gardenias or flowers matching the color of our dress). We always stayed with our date for dances, but socialized at the tables surrounding the dance floor. As the dance went on, uncomfortable heels were kicked off, jackets hung lifeless on the chairs, and ties loosened, and we began really enjoying the night. When the last song played and the dim lights were brightened, we knew it was time to find our "wraps" (or jackets) in the cloak room and finish the evening at a restaurant or drive-in.

Which place to eat was usually the choice of the person driving. I remember one time, one of our fathers elected to pick us up and take us out to eat after the dance. He sat in the bar while we reviewed the menu, shocked at the prices. He had chosen an eating place that was out of our price range, but not to fear, ingenuity prevailed. One couple shared a plate of spaghetti with a Coke, another couple enjoyed the free glasses of water with lemon and munched on the free bread sticks, and the third couple ordered the cheapest meal at this well-known Italian restaurant and shared it with the rest of us. It wasn't the drive-in our dates were expecting, but it was a story to tell.

One evening at the Peony Park Ballroom was especially wonderful. Your Baba Herk was a second-year student at Duchesne College, and your great-grandmother, Lill, told me to come home early because we had plans. I knew it was my sister's prom night, so I looked forward to being a part in her preparation for the dance. She had purchased a full-length, light-pink dress that hung attractively around her thin frame. Her date for the night had given her a wrist corsage of white roses, and she had her blond hair twisted up into a French twist with large bangs and sprinkles of white glitter. What a vision; she looked like a queen, and Mom and I had such fun dressing our queen.

Sometime during the preparatory hours, my mom drew me into a private room and shared that Bert had been chosen to be Prom Queen by her classmates, and it was a secret. She and her date were dancing as Dad, Mom, and I hid ourselves out of sight at one of the back tables. I was sneaking around, hiding myself from view, hating to use the bathroom for fear I would be detected and give away the secret. Halfway through the night, Eddy Haddad's trumpets flourished, announcing the time had come to reveal the Queen and King of the Prom. She and her King walked down the aisle to their crowning. She looked beautiful, and I was so happy for her surprise. But as it happened, the surprise was mine, because everyone in our family knew but me—including Bert!

This magic park had such wonderful memories for me. But years later, Peony Park lost its luster as the city of Omaha munched at the surrounding land and surrounded it with commercial buildings, tracks of identical-looking homes, traffic, lights, taxation, and new demands.

A struggling Peony Park faced with loss of attendance, put in a children's amusement park, which
was semi-successful at first, but soon found stiff

competition with family fun spots that were mush-rooming in the city.

Other variables came into play, affecting the downfall of the park. Maintenance was not a major priority now, and much of the greenery was cut down to allow new park activities. The pool bathhouse seemed to lack its usual clean appearance, and nationally known bands did not come as frequently for the ballroom dancers of Omaha. The '50s were also a time of segregation of Blacks in Omaha businesses, and as we moved toward the desegregation of the early '60s, Peony Park was required to allow Blacks (or Negroes as they were called then) into the facilities. I did not even realize this inequity existed until it was made public, and sadly, integration was reported to have affected attendance. Bankruptcy loomed, and eventually the property had to be divided into sections and sold to commercial businesses—so sad.

Sports, Speech, and Drama

All Omaha schools, especially Catholic schools in the '50s, had fierce rivalries. Cathedral's main rival in sports was Holy Name High School, and each year the cheerleaders and administration would pump up the pep club to decorate cars, buy pennants and crepe paper and paint, and make signs for the parade to the game. Long before our decorated cars turned into the football parking lot, our cheers of "VICTORY, VICTORY THAT'S OUR CRY. V-I-C-T-O-R-Y, ARE WE IN IT? WELL, I GUESS. CATHEDRAL HIGH SCHOOL, YES! YES! YES!" announced the arrival of the Cathedral supporters.

The boys on the team, coaches, and their other male helpers had arrived much earlier for the warm-up exercises, but they could hear the loud, feminine cheering voices of the pep club calling for a victory. Why were the voices mainly female? Because there were no sports for girls, and the girls' job was to support the boys. Although I thought cheerleading was a sport, it did not have a competitive edge. I was surprised to find in high school, the only girl competition was a volleyball or basketball game during gym class or on field days, (and anytime a girl wanted to skip either, she simply had to claim that she had "cramps," and she could sit on the bench—easy peesy). Females were too fragile back then, it seemed, for heavy duty competition.

Where females could compete was Speech and Drama under the auspices of Sister C. As a member of her speech team, this hard-working Dominican sister walked into your extracurricular life, your after-school life, and for some into their love life, anything interfering with your speech responsibilities.

Sister C. sent debate teams by train as far as Minneapolis or Chicago to compete in regional competitions. The National Forensic League membership became the "letter sweater" for the girls that participated in speech. Her young and older teams hosted and attended competitions throughout our area.

We practiced extemporaneous, humorous, and dramatic presentations after school at our house in preparation for speech contests throughout the city. I spent as much time practicing my pieces in front of the bathroom mirror as being critiqued by Sister C. By contest time, my entire family could all recite by heart "Yertle the Turtle" (by Doctor Seuss), humorous category, or the "The Snow Goose" (by Paul Gallico) in the dramatic category, or my original oration my senior year. Most of Sister C's students qualified to compete at state speech and many times placed or won. Cathedral Speech was successful under her direction.

Extemporaneous speaking and debate had the real stars. As underclassmen, we watched upperclass ladies and men bring home the "gold" (medals and trophies) from each tournament in which they competed. Creighton Prep was my personal nemesis in debate, but Skip, George and I won in other contests throughout the city, so we remained on the team. Extemporaneous speaking was my challenge, but I was never successful.

Speaking only from my research notes called for a self-confidence I did not have, and I left the extemporaneous team.

Sister C. helped each member of her speech team succeed, but she also gave up on my extempt endeavor. It was no wonder she had a winning speech team. She was always bumping into our classes with arms full of boxes of pamphlets, magazines, books, past winning speeches, and poems for us. With her help in 1960, my original oratory competition took me to State and earned a third-place win.

He Ain't Heavy, Father, He's My Brother

C ars and vehicles became more important to the American family in the 1950s, almost a necessity. Our father, Bob Kauth, loved cars. Our driveway always sported a waxed, spotless, second-hand beauty, and we shared his pride. Years earlier as a suitor to our mother, Lillian Pease, who lived on the corner of 44th and Dodge (a busy road, even in the 1930s), he would drive up in his shiny, convertible coup with the top down and a friend in the rumble seat for their skating date. The highly waxed surface and its good-looking driver made your great-grandmother call him a "handsome picture," and he won her heart.

When Bert and I were young, air conditioning in cars or homes did not exist, and cars played a major part in our cooling off in the hot Midwestern summers.

For example, on a hot evening, many times we would
pile into the family car and drive to the small town
of Irvington, just outside of Omaha, known for
its wonderful ice cream shop. Hot summer nights
were also cooled when the family popped popcorn,
bought a six pack of Coke and went to an outdoor
drive-in theater to watch a movie on the huge screen
and enjoy the summer breezes. On the weekends,
we enjoyed picnics and trips to surrounding sandpits and lakes. Louisville and Cowles Lakes were just
south of Omaha, and Fremont and Valley Sandpits
were north and were often our destinations for
water play. The family car was an important part in
surviving Midwestern heat in those days.

Even in the winter, cars were a part of our entertainment. Advent before Christmas was not Advent without our slow, family ride through the Dundee and Underwood neighborhoods, then West Omaha. Bert and I would jump from one side of the back seat to the other side trying not to miss any of the brightly lit Christmas displays and tall pine trees bedecked with large, multi-colored bulbs. Seat belts were not a facet of car safety then, so the fight for the best window brought corrective comments from the parents in the front seat.

Television was a new entertainment form in the 1940s and 1950s household, but when the programming from the only functioning three networks became routine, our family would take a road trip out of town just for the ride. Our usual path followed the tracks of the electric street cars that serviced Dodge Street travelers at that time. We would follow the tracks to 72nd Street where the rails stopped, turned around and headed eastward, but our journey would continue west into corn fields and pastures dotted with grazing cattle and pigs. The four lane, cement Dodge Street turned into a two-lane paved highway and was called West Dodge Road.

The welcome smell of sweet grass would blow in the open car windows. The forty-five mile an hour speed limit allowed breezes to enter our back seat and fly out again. Whiffs of the breezes would take out the smoke coming from the Chesterfield cigarettes in the front seat into freedom. Both parents, as most adults then, were smokers, and Bert and I would innocently breathe in the second-hand smoke before it flew out the open window. No one was aware of its dangers back then.

Our trek usually took us to what was a turn-around spot for us, but a very special place for boys who needed a home: Boys Town. Our parents would tell us about this home for boys, fifteen miles outside of the Omaha city limits, and its beginnings with Father Flanagan.

Father Flanagan was a holy Catholic priest, our parents said, who started housing homeless boys from the Omaha streets during the Depression.

Originally he housed the original eight home-less boys in the rectory, but the number of boys needing homes increased, and requests began to come. A large piece of land west of Omaha was bequeathed to the Father and his mission, and things began to change.

He and the boys developed a village on the new land with a constitution, a school and a post office. The boys eventually governed themselves with an elected mayor and village council. Father developed the Boys Town Choir, and the young voices appeared throughout the country in concert, which became another source of revenue. Through church assistance, donations, and income from choir appearances, streets were paved, buildings built, and volunteers turned into paid staff.

When our father became friends with a Boys Town priest in the '50s, we understood better how Boys Town had changed throughout the years. At that time, boys came from all over the country in numbers, and though once simply an orphanage, it had now become a residential program with house mothers and fathers governing the dormitories. Although eventually Boys Town accepted girls in their numbers, but in the 1950s they only accepted boys. Their educational system was academic and technical at that time, and they had a fully functioning farm, manned by the boys that providing food for the campus. Most of their needs were met on campus. They did not leave or go into Omaha unless they were going for health reasons, to raise funds for the village, or for earned privileges.

"Father A." was our father's priest friend, and through this friendship, our home became what Father A. called, "the Boys Town in town." The Kauth home became unofficially a small part of the reward system for those boys whose behavior earned a Saturday in Omaha. Father A. would fill his red Ford Mustang convertible with the boys who earned the privilege and bring them to a movie at the downtown Omaha Paramount or State Theater. When the movie was over, the boys would take a bus to 44th and Dodge Street and walk three blocks to our home. Our mother would cook a big pot of something delicious, and we would stuff ourselves. We always enjoyed those Saturday afternoons and hated to see Father A. repopulate his convertible and drive off to the village.

Boys Town had dances and buses that would collect the girls who had been invited. Bert attended more of the dances in the gym than me, but they were fun dances. My best memory of the Boys Town dances were the proms, and one year, my date was Mayor Pat (a Boys Town senior who was elected by his community—quite an honor). It was an arranged date, and we had not met before the dance. I don't know who was more nervous— him or me.

The open-door policy fostered by the Kauth adults extended beyond graduation for both the boys and our family. Boys Town fellas that were a part of the Saturday family ritual visited our home long after graduation. They brought their future brides and their small toddlers or their new cars, sharing the joys of their grown-up lives, as well as their sadness with broken marriages, lost jobs, or loves. The revolving door Father A. and the Boys Town boys enjoyed in our home brought everyone joy throughout the years. By welcoming others to their table and their hearts, our parents showed their children and our community that people weren't a burden, they were our brothers.

Boys Town did not leave our radar in later years either. After your great-grandmother (Lill) died, Bob married his high school sweetheart, Catherine, who also had a connection to Father Flanagan. Her mother reported that Catherine was carried as an infant by Father Flanagan in outstretched arms to the baptismal font of the South Omaha church. She also said that her mother sewed clothes for the boys and collected cast-off toys from the parish members. Beyond our stepmother's connection, I personally saw the extension of Father Flanagan's plan for the "Village of Little Men" when I taught at Boys Town while I was getting a master's degree at the University of Nebraska at Omaha.

Boys Town had changed from the dormitory structure to family-run homes on campus and use a behavior modification program. The Boys Town of 2000 not only provided the necessities of life for the boys, but also taught social skills, family living skills and included girls in their numbers. To this day, it provides an excellent scholastic education for boys *and* girls from broken homes, off the streets, or from the courts. The city of Omaha had slowly grown and surrounded the original plot of land, and Boys Town administration had sold some of the original land to banks and businesses. Also, new Boys Town villages are now developing in a number of cities throughout the country.

My admiration for the Boys Town regime grew the more contact I had with it. I fell in love with the students and the faculty and enjoyed my classroom, substituting and summer school sessions. I taught whenever I could, and even constructed a reading and writing syllabus for sessions directed by my old friend who was the reading director for the school. My graduation from UNL at Omaha stopped my frequent visits to Omaha and, sadly, my teaching time at Boys Town. But the Boys Town model and its teaching strategies marched on with me in my teaching career. Father Flanagan would never have guessed how his original plan had blossomed or that someday he would be beatified and in line for sainthood.

MISBEHAVING IN THE 1950S AND THE POLICE

The behavior that we thought was naughty or bad in the 1950s pales in comparison with the youth's misbehavior of the twenty-first century. In the Dominican-ruled empire, very few of us were brave enough to fully partake in the "sins" of that time: drugs, alcohol, or sex. Fear of addiction, social diseases and pregnancy, damnation to hell, and worst yet, disappointing our family stopped most of us from joining in full participation in these activities.

Somehow during the evolution of our consciences tutored by the Catholic regime and the Dominican sisters, rigid awareness had been built in our psyche to avoid these dangers and pleasures. Oh, most of us probably experimented at some level with all three of these, but for my circle of friends, and perhaps I can speak for the majority of my fellow students, the use or participation in any of these activities was occasional. Even with our public school peers, alcohol was probably the drug of choice. Hard drugs were not that popular with most, nor was their acquisition easy in the '50s, and beer was easy to get. Sex was probably the most available for all students, but our fears usually prevented full participation.

The priests and sisters were themselves bound by vows of celibacy, and the frequent "fire and brimstone" sermons to teens from the pulpit always somehow ended up discussing the "sins of the flesh." The only three classes in school that even closely approached the topic of sex were Religion Class (taught by a celibate priest or nun), Home Economics (preparing a young girl for marriage and a Catholic home), and Biology (looking scientifically at the bodily function of reproduction). In the pathway to graduation, these classes were required at Cathedral and were deemed as enough information by the religious to prepare us for our lives as sexual creatures.

We were actually well prepared for the celibacy they were hoping we were practicing. Girls were made especially aware of the dangers of pregnancy, disease, and the condemnation by her family, school, and church. Birth control was a sin and never mentioned, as they believed that the best means of controlling births was controlling yourself. However, they also taught that in marriage, it was a sin for a wife to ever say no to her husband.

Petting and "French kissing," they told us, were avenues to the loss of this control, and the sisters were vigilant in watching for signs of these activities. Hickies (sucked bruises on the neck) was one sign that alerted them. Another red flag was wearing items that belonged to your boyfriend or girlfriend. When the judgment on going out exclusively with one boy or girl or possible intimacy was made, the student was counseled, and if the problem was not corrected, the real powerhouse, the parents, were called into the discussion. All of this scrutiny was in the name of protecting us.

From the pulpit we were often warned of committing "sins of the flesh," and in the classroom, we heard about scary social diseases. I remember those ugly pictures on overhead projectors, and they alone scared many girls from "going all the way" (our euphemism for sex). All of these strategies did help many a Catholic girl walk down the aisle under her virginal veils, proclaiming her purity.

What did we do for fun, you may ask? Actually we were seldom at a loss for a good time. In every group of friends, someone had a car or could borrow their family car, and we would pool our money, buy gas, and head out for the Friday ritual.

Dodge Street, the main artery of Omaha at that time, became a very slow procession of cars and teenagers every Friday night, socializing from one food drive-in (Burger King on 78th) in what was then West Omaha to another (Tiners on 44th) in mid-Omaha. The Omaha police would sit silently in the shadows, waiting for some kid-problem to arise. Without their vigilance, drag races would develop down Dodge Street, disregarding red lights and stop signs, but in their presence, the racers would drive slowly while observing all the rules. Reaching the drive-in parking area, we would move bumper to bumper through both fast food places in a snake-like line, observing who was there, and waving and shouting to our parked friends.

The drive-in managers set rules to keep the food-selling business going with all of this socialization. We could only keep our parking place if an order came in periodically through the two-way microphone hanging on the side of each car. Our order was delivered to our car by a hired kid, probably saving for his own car. Cherry Coke and an order of French fries would be shared by the whole car, and then it was time to join the snake line again and wiggle our way to the next order of Coke, fries, and friends at Burger King at the other end of Dodge Street.

My dad bought an old convertible Studebaker, "Hoopie" we called her. Her design resembled a spaceship, and some former owners actually placed a spinner on the front point of the grille. What a great car!

It was just for fun use, however, never to be used for riding to school. Only students from outside the parish were allowed to drive cars to Cathedral. So, even though my walk to school in all types of weather was about twelve blocks uphill with my little sister tagging behind, my little car luxuriated in the driveway, awaiting my return. I loved my "Hoopie," and Dad let me use it for Dodge Street rituals and transportation to speech activities and dances.

When we didn't have a date on the weekends, driving to dances or sporting events all over the city allowed socialization with other teens. In South Omaha there were ethnic dance groups that invited teens to participate, and in the small towns surrounding Omaha (Plattsmouth and Louisville), teen halls with food and music attracted city kids too. We also enjoyed watching our favorite boy sports at a variety of schools, and cheerleaders and the Pep Club members organized parades, floats, costumes, face painting, and car decorating, which always ended in a dance.

Ice skating and roller skating were other fun ways to fill our time in the '50s. In the winter, we ice skated indoors and out. Our Kauth grandparents lived in old South Omaha, which was known for woods and hollows (a wooded depression in the land that the city flooded). In the '50s, the deepest part of the hollows stayed frozen all winter, and we could ice skate every weekend when we visited our grandparents on South 16th Street. We hated to skate after a group of boys tore up the ice with their hockey skates, which caused our figure skates to trip on the holes they put in the ice. Later, I learned that the hockey culprits probably were your grandpa Ken and his brothers because they grew up right around the block from our grandparents and played hockey in the same hollow.

We also enjoyed AKSARBEN (Nebraska spelled backwards), another large piece of land originally outside the Omaha city limits, housing many activities. Horse racing for the adults and traveling carnivals for the family were popular activities on the property, but the AKSARBEN community center also housed a wide variety of other activities for the people of Omaha. The community arena housed an ice rink (the only inside rink at that time) that was available for the public and for the more serious skaters training in figure and freestyle skating. The auditorium hosted rodeos, conventions, and civic activities when there was no ice, but an all-time favorite was the annual AKSARBEN ball with a king (usually a well-known Omaha business man) and a queen (usually the young daughter of a prominent Omaha family). The Aksarben board was able to transform the same auditorium from a stinky, smelly straw-filled rodeo arena to the regal palace of the Kingdom of Quivera to an ice-skating rink in short time, and Omaha loved it.

My friend C. took the sport of ice skating more seriously than I did with 4:30 a.m. coaching sessions and rented ice space for practice. No 4:30s for me, but I went as often as I could later in the day. I got to enjoy lots of skating time when I went with her. She ended up skating for the Ice Capades and toured Russia and Europe, and I ended up teaching kids in a classroom.

She and I also roller skated, and since I had been doing that since I was three years old, I was glad to find a partner my age in my sport. My mother and father (Bob Kauth and Lill Pease) had met at the Farnam Roller Bowl, and my dad introduced me to the sport when he made skates for me out of baby shoes. Both parents skated well and resembled the "Old Smoothies" of Ice Capade fame.

FARNAM ROLLER NEWS

VOL. I   JUNE 1947   NO. 5

WEST FARNAM ROLLER RINK   EDITED AND PUBLISHED BY PAULA DOLNER

My friend C. was really good at both sports, trained with coaches, and became competitive and successful. I enjoyed skating with her at both rinks. Her skates were handcrafted, but mine were a sale item at Sears, but they both worked, and we had fun.

A "naughty" activity at that time and one that almost got your grandma thrown out of Cathedral, involved toilet paper from home, towels from the local gas stations, napkins from the local drive ins, and any political or lawn sign that was removable. It was the famous "TP" activity. We would case the victim's (always a friend) yard several days before the crime. The more trees in the yard the better because the toilet paper would drape from one limb to another and develop a Christmas tree appearance. Yard lights and appliances were good too, because they would become glowing white pieces of art with toilet paper bows and streamers illuminating their light and giving a mystic sense to the endeavor. With a toss of individual napkins and towels taken from the local gas station rest rooms, they would rise into the dark sky from our toss and flutter like a Colorado snow covering the ground. The last installment was the stolen signs, begging the election of any politician, placed anywhere and everywhere there was space. We felt we left each yard a unique wonderland of white.

Our work of art, however, was not always appreciated by the recipients of the deed nor the school administration, and our last TP job even involved disapproval of the Omaha police. This incident involved a wonderful, tree-filled yard of an Air Force colonel, a carload of leftover TP materials, and a strong desire of loving revenge.

My friend and I had elected not to go to a Criss Cross Dance, a fund raiser at Peony Park for the Red Cross, and all of our close friends went. Instead, we decided to TP the houses of those who went, so the collection of materials had to begin several weeks before the crime. Visits to public bathrooms gave us handfuls of individual toilet napkins, and we visited every public bathroom up and down Dodge Street so they would not suspect. Our parents also never noticed the disappearance of the extra rolls of toilet paper from the closet when we took them slowly, nor did the local diners suspect the disappearance of the napkins from their aluminum boxes that sat on each table. It was election year, so our collection of signs and election pamphlets was huge after a few weeks of slow pilfering.

Only two girls were attempting to complete this big task before midnight, so we had to move quickly. When the dark fell, we reared our loaded car into action, ready for the mission, and moved out. Excitement built as we quickly worked at the tasks in the yards of our friends who were dancing the night away, unaware of our devious behavior.

The routine was always the same. We quickly threw the rolls of toilet paper to the other person on the opposite side of the tree allowing the "decoration" to fall from the overhead limbs to the ground like white Christmas boughs. When all of the trees were sporting their new outfits, we tossed the individual tissues and cards in the air to make a snow-like covering on the lawn, followed by expert placement of political signs around the yard. Any fences, pets, and lanterns stimulated special creative treatments. Satisfaction of each yard moved us on to the next.

The midnight curfew appeared before we had completed the last house, the home in Dundee of an Air Force colonel stationed at SAC (Strategic Air Command). His son had gone to the Criss Cross Dance with one of our friends, and we had intended to TP (toilet paper) his home the night of the dance as well but couldn't, so we vowed to complete the task at a later date.

Toilet tissue and signs were left for this home, and other Cathedral students had volunteered to help us TP his house, so once dark settled, that next weekend, we were in Dundee, searching the fronts of the large brick homes for the correct address. Bingo, we found it. Quietly we began the decoration process; oh, and such lovely pine trees stood in their front yard. This bunch of toilet-paper artists were so intent upon their work, they did not at first notice the police were quietly approaching the villains committing the crime.

Once the presence of the police was discovered, however, our work crew resembled roaches escaping a kitchen light. My co-conspirator and I were too late in running, so we jumped under one of the beautiful pines. Pine needles digging into our legs and arms, low pine limbs cracking us on our heads, and pine cones biting our knees in retaliation as we crawled on them to the center of the tree did not bring a cry or sigh, just giggles from us fugitives. We quietly watched, through the toilet paper boughs, the black shadows of our friends being chased by a police car with its swirling red cherry top light. They collected our fleeing comrades and took them to jail, while my friend and I sat silently in the belly of our pine tree waiting for the quiet of the night to resume.

An all-school assembly was called on Monday before classes were dismissed, and we were all directed to the auditorium. I walked slowly down the hall and through the double doors next to the stage, and my jaw dropped. On the stage were the administration of the school and parish and all of the TP work crew facing the audience—including my co-conspirator! Why was I not a part of the disciplinary flagging that followed? Had no one told on me?

Guilt flooded into my every cell as the principal and superintendent took turns ranting and railing about what we had done, and my convicted comrades faced the school's disappointment and anger alone. Once my friends' scouring eyes found the missing sinner in the audience, their eyes seemed to burn holes through me. The administration claimed that expulsion was possible, and further legal action was probable by Colonel Whomever since we had damaged his property (with toilet paper ?). Although I was drowning in my guilt, sitting among the innocents, when the bell rang at the end of the tirade deriding my co-conspirators, I dissolved into the crowd, rushing to dismissal and appearing as innocent as I could as I ran home unscathed but feeling really dirty. I think an upcoming speech tournament in which I was to compete and Sister C. had saved me, but I am not sure. The other offenders only had their fear as their punishment, no jail, no suspension, no clean-up duty, just threats happened.

Our class was also somewhat mischievous in the classroom. Tricks we played on the teachers are a fun subject for reunions. Students often chuckle with the story of setting the classroom alarm clock of a slightly deaf English teacher each day in eighth period, giving us a fifteen-minute early dismissal each day. Only an alert neighboring teacher stopped our fun, but we enjoyed early dismissal for quite some time. Another giggle provoker involved placement of ugly specimens from the science lab in teachers' drawers and chairs. This was preferable to the old-time tricks of tacks and nails on the teacher's chair, and no one was hurt by a dissected eyeball. Forging parental notes, explaining our inability to wear our uniform, often happened, and we also may have fudged on the number of times we had run around the gym as directed by the P.E. coach who had been distracted. We always worked as a pack; one or two students would divert the coach/or teacher's attention, which allowed the others to perform the devious deed.

These classroom shenanigans were not too common because of the punishment of being *sent to the office* and what happened therein. It seemed to stop a lot of action, and you never wanted Sister mad at you, as lingering consequences were possible. Our fears for the most part were delusional, but they were real in our minds at the time and usually changed our behavior. If it did not change things, out came the big guns—our parents—who always supported the Sisters and administration, so any transgression could become bigger than the classroom or principal's office.

READY OR NOT

At the turn of the New Year, 1960, strange changes began to happen in our class. A once grade-driven group, we were now showing some bad habits. Truancy became common with some, and we began to congregate more often on the large front porch of the school with a deaf ear to the tardy bell. Rules previously followed without question were questioned. Assignments were lost, incomplete, or completely overlooked, and tests were not getting their usual preparation. We were done and far too soon; we had a very bad case of senioritis.

Every trick our teachers tried to combat this attitude, now rolled off our backs rather than alerting us to the fact we were on the last lap to graduation. Many of us had plans that demanded good grade averages, but year-end grades had to be summarized with a flexible approach, so our new behavior would not destroy our hard-earned averages.

Once again, the teachers were befuddled, but they knew to give us our rein and constructed activities that worked to keep us involved. Teachers utilized the practice field next to the school, making it a hot bed of activity with our monitoring contests between individual classes, between classes and faculty, and field day activities of the elementary school. The Home Economics class had a tea honoring the senior class, and we also had an all-school honor assembly for all scholastic, sports, music, and speech awards throughout the year. The sisters tried to make each day different from the ordinary school day with different activities, a little more interesting than the usual Latin or chemistry class.

That spring before graduation moved as slowly as the summer wait before our first grade and Sister Mineve, but the appearance of our rental caps and gowns shook us into reality; we were here, really here, about to graduate.

Trying on our new garb and practicing the long walk up the main aisle of the church and up onto the altar reminded us that everything was changing. We had no idea of what was coming. Even those that had committed to a college were unsure of what that really meant. Those of us who had jobs weren't sure we would be doing them for long.

We just knew we were saying goodbye to our daily routines, our good friends, our so-so friends, the teachers we liked, the teachers we teased, the parking lot in which we used to gather, and the classrooms to which we dashed for the last four years. The closer we came to that graduation night in the church, the more that little group of twenty-three first-grade students, now 110 in number, realized we were leaving what had been our stability for so long and were going to once again have to step into the unknown.

Our graduation Mass was complete, diplomas decreed, and it was time for us to walk back down that beautiful parquet aisle, through the big opening doors, to our freedom, our unknown. As this thought filled my mind, my fear subsided as I realized I was not alone in this. I had all the love two parents could muster to assist me, and each one of those teachers that had been on my journey had given gifts that would walk with me in what was beyond those bronze doors.

God had bestowed so many gifts to us at St. Cecilia's. Sister Mary Mineve had taught me the wonder of good hugs and appreciation of the little things. Mrs. Swan taught me how to be ingenious and caring. Sister Mary Mauritius taught me how to share and build self-esteem (my own and others). Sister Mary Viola taught me fun and diligence in my work. Mrs. Welsh taught me patience and the love of a good story. Sister Mary Adrian taught me how to support each task with love and hard work.

Sister Mary Constantine gave me intellectual challenge and the skills to speak in front of others. Sister Mary Felicia showed me spontaneity. Bonnie Pryor showed me how to have self-control and direction. Sister Mary Amanda taught me resourcefulness and application of self to a difficult task. Sister Mary Lionel taught me creative thinking and flexibility. Sister Mary Lucretia taught spontaneity and kind treatment of others. I found comfort in realizing that each and every teacher, named or not, had been given gifts to be shared with us that we would use in that unknown world beyond those doors. With gratitude for these strengths I was given as a Catholic student in the 1950s, I double stepped down that aisle to what lay ahead.